The Fourth Industrial Revolution and Education

The Fourth Industrial Revolution and Education

Digital Language Learning and Teaching

A compendium of the TESOL-MALL Graduate Program Symposium
and KOTESOL DCC Workshop

Edited by

David Kent

Copyright © 2019.
All rights reserved.

No part of this publication may be reproduced, distributed, or transmitted in any form or by any means, including photocopying, recording, or other electronic or mechanical methods, without prior written permission, except in the case of brief quotations embodied in critical reviews and certain other noncommercial uses permitted by copyright law.

Author Copyright: The author(s) of each chapter retain the copyright to their respective works, permission has been granted to the publisher by the author(s) to reproduce their work in this format.

Distributable Content: The author(s) of each chapter, and the publisher, grant permission for the copy and distribution of handouts and photocopiable material from the book for any and all instructional purposes.

Trademark Notice: Product or corporate names may be trademarks or registered trademarks, and are used only for identification and explanation without intent to infringe.

Cover Artwork: © David Kent

Although every precaution has been taken to verify the accuracy of the information contained herein, the editor and publisher assume no responsibility for any errors or omissions. No liability is assumed for damages that may result from the use of information contained within.

ISBN: 9781925555455

 A catalogue record for this book is available from the National Library of Australia

Pedagogy Press. Sydney, Australia.
www.pedagogypress.com

First Edition.

DEDICATION

*For the students and alumni of the
TESOL-MALL graduate program at Woosong University.*

CONTENTS

Acknowledgments		ix
Preface		xi
1.	Teaching in the Time of Digital Language Learning	1
	David Kent	
2.	Chatbots as Conversational Agents in the Context of Language Learning	32
	Daniel Bailey	
3.	Practical and Innovative Applications for Wikis in a Language Classroom	42
	Michael Cary	
4.	Keep Talking and Nobody Explodes: A Commercial Video Game with EFL Implications	79
	Andrew Aguiar and Nicole Shiosaki	
5.	Explain Everything in the English Classroom	102
	Dilbar Shermatova	
6.	Language Teaching and Technology: A less-is-more Approach to Integration in the Classroom	130
	Natasha Reddy	
7.	Instructor Preference of Cloud-Based Platform and Quiz Type for Formative Assessment	144
	Irada Gezalova	
8.	Exploring the Purdue Online Writing Lab (OWL) and a Flipped Approach: An Integration which Complements Language Learning	163
	Ariadne Patricia Borges	
9.	Will English Remain a Lingua Franca in the Industry 4.0 Era?	182
	Wu Yang (Miranda Wu)	
Glossary		220

ACKNOWLEDGMENTS

I wish to extend my deepest appreciation to my wife *Hyunhee* who has been very patient and understanding throughout the entire process involved with the production of this book, and the instigation, coordination, and running of the associated symposium from which these chapters originate. I would also like to thank *Noel David* for his suggestions regarding this text and for his patience.

PREFACE

The Four Industrial Revolutions

Steam power, which emerged in the 1780s, took over from water-, wind-, horse-, and man-power for driving machines, and this ushered in the rise of the first industrial revolution, and made humans more productive (Gleason, 2018).

The 1870s brought with it the second industrial revolution (Gleason, 2018), and this coincided with the rise of mass production and electrical energy, seeing changes to the ways we live and work, and making humans mobilize to cities, thus increasing urbanization.

In the later part of the 20th century, the development of information technology (IT) and electronics led to the rise of the third industrial revolution, and to the automation of physical strength and manual labor (Brybjolfsson & McAfee, 2014). This enabled more efficient production, and also brought with it access to computing and the internet – forever changing how humans interact with each other.

The fourth industrial revolution, emerging from manufacturing industries in the early 2000s (Gleason, 2018) and bringing with it cyber-physical systems (CPS) and the second machine age (Rajkumar, Lee, Sha, & Stankovic, 2010), stems from increasing computing capacity, the development of mass storage of big data and its analyses, AI (artificial intelligence) and machine learning, and the networking of machines with the Internet of Things (IoT). This has made humans increasingly reliant on CPS, and this has brought with it a shift to the automation of knowledge. Schwab (2017) highlights that the fourth industrial era, along with CPS, will permanently come to alter and disrupt the ways in which we live and work. Arguably too, it will come to permanently change how and why we will learn, how and when we will teach, and how and what we will study.

Rationale for the Text

The core of this text aims to cover the use and applicability of various technologies and applications specifically presented and examined for educational advantage in the era of the fourth industrial revolution, and its use with 21st century learners. Taken into consideration is the changing learning and teaching landscape of this era, and the importance of assessing the usability, implementation, and evaluation of the technological tools that any instructor (or learner) might choose to use. Also explored are the potential place of the English language and the changing needs of how and why it needs to be learned.

Keeping the above in mind, this book is aimed at those instructors who are teaching English to speakers of other languages (TESOL) in the English as a foreign language (EFL) context, but it is also worthwhile for any English as a second language (ESL) instructor. It is also an essential read for any educator, student, administrator, or stakeholder involved with the TESOL industry, particularly those who want to understand how pre-service and in-service teachers are honing their technological teaching craft, and how digital language learning and teaching currently, and will potentially, impact the educational sector.

Of significance, content has been specifically developed by both native and non-native English language pre- and in-service language teachers to encompass a variety of possibilities, theories, methods, and approaches, as well as a diversity of pedagogical and linguistic outcomes suitable to a wide range of teaching and learning contexts. These include that of young learners through to young adults, and all those undergoing life-long learning. This text also gives voice to the work of certificate and masters students of the TESOL-MALL graduate program and doctoral students of the Endicott College of International Studies at Woosong University in the Republic of Korea. Through the text, these students are being granted the opportunity to have their first symposium presentations published as chapters four through eight. For most, this will be their first ever publication, and it is hoped that seeing their work in print will come to encourage these emerging scholars, filling them with confidence, and seeing them eager to seek out and conduct further study and/or engage in any research opportunities that the future might afford.

Organization of the Text

The book consists of nine chapters, and it is intended to be read as a whole or in part; by teachers, students, parents, professors, administrators, and any other stakeholders who may be interested in the topics.

In chapter one, *Teaching in the time of digital language learning*, Associate Professor David Kent, Head of the TESOL-MALL graduate program at Woosong University in the Republic of Korea, discusses the impact of the rise of the fourth industrial revolution on education, the impact of digital language learning and teaching, and the importance of assessing the usability, implementation, and evaluation of technological tools for use in instruction. Conceptual frameworks are presented, and a rubric is provided to help instructors and learners analyze any technologies that they might seek to use with their learners in the industry 4.0 era.

Chapters two through eight focus on presenting aspects of the pedagogy behind various methods and approaches that teachers and students can use when relying on technological tools for instruction and student engagement, and to present models of diverse techniques that can assist students in practicing and perfecting their English language skills as they develop the core competencies and skills that they require as learners today.

Chapter two, *Chatbots as conversational agents in the context of language learning*, sees Assistant Professor Daniel Bailey (Konkuk University Glocal Campus) discuss the role of conversational agents in the EFL/ESL context. He posits that such agents can be relied upon to assist students in overcoming writing challenges by engaging them in writing (typing skill) practice that is based upon role play, storytelling, and simulated text messaging.

In chapter three, *Practical and innovative applications for wikis in the language classroom*, Assistant Professor Michael Cary (Kyonggi University – Main Campus, Suwon) examines the potential behind the development of a wiki, and the roles that wikis can play in foreign language education.

Andrew Aguiar and Nicole Shiosaki, alumni of the TESOL-MALL graduate program at Woosong University, examine the role of gamification in chapter four, with particular emphasis on the application of one particular video game – *Keep talking and nobody explodes: A commercial video game with EFL implications*. The chapter highlights the potential for gamification to see students interact with each other in meaningful ways when they might otherwise not.

In chapter five, Dilbar Shermatova, a recent Master of Arts graduand of the TESOL-MALL graduate program at Woosong University, discusses the place of interactive whiteboard applications in engaging students in the learning process, with a focus on *Explain Everything in the English classroom*. Attention revolves around how this application can be exploited in novel and interesting ways for developing student-centered interactive activities and for providing language learning opportunities.

Natasha Reddy, a Master of Arts student in the TESOL-MALL graduate program and an Assistant Professor in the Woosong University Language Institute, in chapter six, *Language teaching and technology: a less-is-more approach to integration in the classroom*, considers reliance upon a few key technologies as a better fit for the EFL classroom over reliance on a multitude. Options for the use of the social messaging service *KakaoTalk* for instructor- and learner-centered teaching and learning approaches then come to the fore.

Chapter seven, *Instructor preference of cloud-based platform and quiz type for formative assessment,* sees Irada Gezalova, a Master of Arts student in the TESOL-MALL graduate program at Woosong University, discuss the preference and satisfaction rates of instructors when using cloud-based platforms for formative assessment. How the most-used question types compare in terms of student accuracy rates when formative assessment is conducted using those platforms is also examined.

Ariadne Patricia Borges, also a Master of Arts student in the TESOL-MALL graduate program at Woosong University, in chapter eight, *Exploring the Purdue OWL (online writing lab) and a flipped approach: An integration which complements language learning,* considers the challenges that teachers and learners face when learning to write in a foreign/second language, and how these can be overcome using online writing labs and a flipped classroom model. She presents an overview for how teachers and students might best acquire and enhance learners' writing skills, strategies, motivation, engagement, and making meaning from experience when using such an approach.

Finally, doctoral candidate Wu Yang (Miranda Wu) in the closing chapter of the book, chapter nine, *Will English remain a lingua franca in the industry 4.0 era?,* considers the future of English and how AI (artificial intelligence) might change the way people use and learn languages. The chapter examines how this kind of disruptive technology, alongside the rise of the economic strength of Mandarin, might come to displace English as a lingua franca during the 21st century.

Ultimately, it is hoped that this book will provide both education and something new for all of those who are interested in the field of TESOL, and the impact that the fourth industrial revolution will hold for teaching in the time of digital language learning.

David Kent

References

Brynjolfsson, E., & McAfee, A. (2014). *The second machine age: Work, progress, and prosperity in a time of brilliant technologies.* New York, USA: W. W. Norton.

Gleason, N. (Ed.). (2018). *Higher education in the era of the fourth industrial revolution.* USA: Palgrave Macmillan.

Rajkumar, R., Lee, I., Sha, L., & Stankovic, J. (2010). Cyber-physical systems: The next computing revolution. In *Proceedings of the 47th Design Automation Conference.* (pp. 731-736). USA: Anaheim, California. https://doi.org/10.1145/1837274.1837461

Schwab, K. (2017). *The fourth industrial revolution.* New York, USA: Crown publishing group.

1. Teaching in the Time of Digital Language Learning

David Kent
Woosong University

Introduction – Impact of the Fourth Industrial Revolution on Education

The fourth industrial revolution has seen the convergence of innovation and technology, led by AI (artificial intelligence), big data, and IoT (the internet of things), and it has restructured industry across all sectors including that of education (Doucet, et al., 2018). These changes have been disruptive, and include how our students interact with us as teachers as well as how we as teachers prepare and provide learning opportunities in and outside of the classroom transform (Warschauer, 2000; Goh, 2015). Moving forward, these changes will also see the need to provide learners with different skill sets, not only ones that they will need to use to function in the classroom, but in society and the workplace as well. For teachers too, it may also lead to changes regarding with 'whom' we will teach, and how best we might begin to integrate robots and AI-based digital assistants into the classroom as teaching aids, and how their value can be harnessed to provide learners with life-long study companions (Kent, 2019). These changes have already seen how we access the content transform, providing perhaps too much with quality that is hard to assess. It therefore becomes imperative that now, more than at any other time, teachers be able to understand what digital language learning means, what the benefits are, and how they can analyze and evaluate any technologies that they might seek to employ with their learners.

The 21st Century Learner Landscape

Long gone are the days of the isolated language learner and the cassette-based language lab; learners are now connected to each other through chat groups and online social media platforms. There is no longer a need to ask a native-speaker for the pronunciation of a word, or for vocabulary definitions or examples of grammar in use. Students can ask AI now. Tapes have been replaced with podcasts and YouTube videos for individuals, DVDs and CDs have been replaced with streaming video and audio in many classrooms, with the content that they house all, available on demand. Digital textbooks are also being delivered alongside online tutoring and just-in-time learning with user generated content, especially that from other teachers being increasingly shared for just-in-time download for class. Thus, there is an ever-increasing availability and access to content, perhaps too much, with quality hard to assess. Of course, too, there are multiple literacies to learn, like digital literacy, computer literacy, media literacy, information literacy, technology literacy, political literacy, cultural literacy, critical literacy, multicultural literacy, biliteracy, global literacy, and visual literacy (to name a handful), and along with all of these, there are digital competencies to master. All of this affords our learners with increased exposure and access to technologies that can increase their availability to content in different ways. In other words, today, learning opportunities have become increasingly interactive, social, and multimodal (Richards, 2015).

Shifting Provisions of Learning

New learning opportunities have brought with them a shift to providing non-linear, modular learning pathways, and personalized learning opportunities for students (Doucet, et al., 2018) that sees the way that we as instructors must teach, provide, assess content, interact with our students, engage with resources, and develop our craft change as well. Examples here include: flipping the classroom; applying bring-your-own-device (BYOD); integrating app use and normalizing technological use; working more and more with digitized content to develop increasingly visual- and multimedia-focused presentations; engaging in computer-mediated communication (CMC) by constructing visually-based digital conversations both synchronously and asynchronously (human-to-human, human-to-machine, and machine-to-human); providing online tutoring; emailing reports; relying on just-in-time downloads for classroom activities; developing data-driven learning by engaging in aspects of concordancing and vocabulary profiling; becoming increasingly exposed to cloud-based learning and teaching techniques; and coping with the gamification of learning and reduced attention spans of learners in a time where they need to develop critical and creative learning skills – all this while perhaps also developing an online virtual personal learning environment (PLE) and coping with the rise and reliance on social media for networking.

Figure 1. Wordle in the shape of hands illustrating the shifting provisions of learning

See Figure 1 for a wordle illustrating these shifting provisions of learning. Recognizably though, inherent within many of these changes is the ever-increasing need for us as teachers to assist learners with their language skill development, whether that be through MOOCs (massive open online courses), online, blended, AI-based, app-based, or face-to-face learning, by relying on the affordances of technology which can be used to provide learners with tailored digital language learning opportunities.

Digital Language Learning (DLL)

At its most basic, digital language learning refers to the application of technology within the teaching and learning process. It is a term that has been used to "embrace all uses of technology in language education" including the integration of the tools, techniques, methodologies, and activities inherited from the research and practice found in Computer Assisted Language Learning (CALL), Multimedia Assisted Language Learning (MALL), Technology-enhanced language learning (TELL), Robot Assisted Language Learning (RALL), and others like computer-mediated communication (CMC) including that between human-to-human, human-to-machine, and machine-to-human (Carrier, 2017). The purpose behind the implementation of digital language learning is to enhance learning and teaching via the opportunities that technology affords, to perhaps provide a means for students to comprehend and utilize content more readily, and to engage in learning more interactively, while leveraging instructor time (MIT, 2016). It is therefore important to understand that any use of technology with students is driven by the pedagogy behind the implementation and not the technology itself.

Digital Language Learning Pedagogy

The learning theories that have been applied to technologies promoting digital language learning cover a wide range and scope, vary according to the purpose behind deployment, and include those such as: activity theory, behaviorism, cognitivism, collaborative learning, connectivism, constructivism, context awareness learning, problem-based learning, navigationism, situated learning, and socio-cultural theory (Keskin & Metcalf, 2011). Some of these learning theories have been long entrenched in the development of digital language learning content (Naismith et al., 2004), and highlights that digital language learning is not as recently emerging as many people may think, as it dates back to the 1960s.

What has changed is our exposure to it in our daily life (the role it has taken); the way we interact with technology (socio-collaboratively); the means of interacting with the technology (environment); and how technology interacts with us (connectivism). In the classroom, this might have been as a tutor (where technology teaches the learner), a tutee (where the learner teaches the computer), a tool (where technology is used to achieve a task), a resource, or a device that helps us to establish a learning environment. So, the way we interact with technology has changed, with it now serving well in helping us to create Communities of Practice or affinity spaces as Gee (2004) calls them, places in which people develop relationships in a discourse community based on their shared interests. For students this might mean offline spaces like the traditional classroom, where they practice English utilizing technology in an interactive, integrated and normalized way, and for native speaking English language teachers working in Korea this might mean online spaces (like the KOTESOL or the TESOL-MALL alumni Facebook groups) where teachers-as-learners can engage in professional development as part of a PLE (personal learning environment). This leads us into connectivism.

Connectivist Learning Theory

Connectivism has been described as a 'learning theory for the digital age' (Siemens, 2005), and it stems from socio-cultural learning theories that argue that learning occurs more effectively when people work together. Not only does connectivism view that learning occurs by engaging with a diversity of ideas and opinions, with new ideas constructed through shared thinking and conversations, but that this knowledge can also reside within machines. Examples are the internet, which is a vast repository of knowledge (perhaps, of variable quality), and WolframAlpha, a computational knowledge engine that relies on curated data (which, by the way, Alexa has access to). It also includes the ways in which people store knowledge within machines, and how they interact with that knowledge and with other humans, as well as AIs (artificial intelligences) like Digital Assistants, in order to take control of their own learning, as they retrieve and engage with knowledge. More basic examples include the use of PowerPoints and interactive whiteboards for presenting and interacting with stored knowledge. So, technology is viewed as a resource, and as a way to mediate human interactions, with these interactions making use of different connections and different language forms depending on the media. Hence, knowing where to find information is more important than knowing that information, with the ability to see connections between fields, ideas, and concepts being a core competency.

The DLL Teaching Model

For instructors we no longer talk about technology replacing teachers, or even teachers who use technology replacing those that do not (Wheeler, 2013), we expect to be incorporating technologies for learning into our classrooms. This means that instructors today need to be able to competently utilize their training and expertise to best apply whatever technologies that they have selected for use within a particular teaching and learning context. They must be able to competently assess and evaluate the suitability and appropriateness of how that technology meets the intended teaching and learning objectives of the activity, course, or lesson in which it is applied, as well as understand all levels of educational potential behind its use, along with assisting learners in being able to identify those elements (Fotos & Brown, 2004; Levy & Stockwell, 2006). In other words, teachers need to develop a digital-language-learning teaching model that incorporates instructor-learner(s), peer-to-peer, learner-to-device, and device-to-learner interaction that is guided and managed by the instructor, along with the integration of in-class and out-of-class activities with appropriate and explicit guidance to content and resources that can best manage learning opportunities for students (Carrier, 2017). At the same time, they are responsible for making judgments of the overall appropriateness and quality of any digital content being applied based on their unique teaching approach, the curriculum being implemented, the learning context, and students' needs. This does not mean that every teacher needs to become a technology expert, but it does require moving from being a 'sage on the stage' to being a 'guide on the side', facilitating language learning along a continuum of choice (see Figure 2), and adopting the affordances and course design components appropriate for digital language learning.

Continuum of Choice
< Teacher-centered → Learner-driven >

Participant	Co-Designer	Designer	Advocate	Entrepreneur
Teacher	*Teacher*	*Learner*	*Learner*	*Learner*
Provides menu of options	Points to options and then gets out of the way	Chooses topics based on interests or questions	Identifies a challenge or problem	Self-regulates learning based on passion and purpose
Provides choices to access, engage and express	Invites input from learners	Identifies ideas for designing	Chooses strategies and people to develop action plans for advocacy	Expands purpose by creating business

Figure 2. Continuum of choice (based on Bray & McClasky, 2017)

These course design components include:
- Ubiquitous learning – anywhere, anytime engagement with content.
- Active knowledge making – the production of authentic content.
- Multimodal meaning – using new media resources that include data sets, links, text, images, sound, and data.
- Recursive feedback – conducting machine-mediated [formative] assessment.
- Collaborative intelligence – learning as a social activity with knowledge formation documented and transparent.
- Metacognition – making meaning.
- Differentiated learning – content according to the needs and interests of each pupil.

DLL Implementation Contexts

Overall, the technologies available and those that can be adapted and incorporated into a given teaching and learning context, once evaluated, will likely be dependent upon the devices that instructors and learners have access to the infrastructure, networking and connectivity options available, and the various regulations and policies put in place by either an organization or a government. This aside, key digital language learning technologies might include those that provide input, interactivity, and portability (Carrier, 2017), and those that are available cost-free. Input technologies would include those such as interactive white boards, overhead projectors, tablets, and virtual reality headsets. Interactive technologies would include any device or software that enables language production and material interaction either individually (e.g., via online quizzes), with peers (e.g., utilizing applications, videoconferencing), or student-teacher interaction (e.g., through student response systems), while portable technologies would include smart phones and tablets (either BYODs which are bring-your-own devices, or those provided to learners). Cost-free technologies include those that are ad-supported as well as those available without payment, and locally installed (like smartphone or tablet applications) or those more widely available websites (such as MOOCs which are massive open online courses, or skills-focused resource-based websites). This also increasingly includes a number of ever sophisticated applications and websites that are well-established, which can potentially be integrated within the teaching and learning context in a variety of ways. See, for example, pages such as the Compleat Lexical Tutor (2019) for tools available to conduct concordancing and vocabulary profiling of student work and texts in order to provide data-driven learning.

Digital Language Learning Integration

Aspects of integration that need to be considered involve the incorporation of the technology into the lesson plan for the development, delivery, or practice of content, as well as interaction methods behind incorporation of the technology into the learning context. For example, will the technology be used to provide new material as part of a primer to the lesson content, presenting or constructing a quiz for either formative or summative assessment purposes, be used by learners to generate new material for language practice, or be implemented for consolidation? And for what part of the lesson (introduction, practice, review), or what purpose (formative or summative assessment)?

Depending on when and how the technology is incorporated to deliver learning content will likely impact on how and who interacts with the technology and when. Technology interaction patterns can mirror other kinds of classroom activity interactions (Lee, 2015), and include that of instructor-to-student and student-to-student communication with collaboration via pair, group, among-group, and whole-class work across offline, online, and blended learning contexts. They can also allow for the student to interact solely with the technology itself.

This all leads to development of in-class versus out-of-class models for knowledge provision (Carrier & Nye, 2016). Language learning classroom examples might include: before-class (reading and listening, text-based study, online vocabulary learning, and/or grammar-in-use activities with applications), in-class (speaking activities, pair work, concept questions, communication activities, games, storytelling, and/or mentoring), and after-class activities (writing, comprehension questions, online workbook use, vocabulary practice with applications, and/or formative assessment).

Analysis & Evaluation of Digital Language Learning Technologies

Although frameworks such as those such as Bloom's Revised digital taxonomy (Kent, 2015) and the SAMR (Puentedura, 2006; Hamilton, Rosenberg, & Akcaoglu, 2016) can be initially useful for teachers to apply, ultimately a shift toward a more intricate means of evaluating and assessing the value of the technological tools being implemented in the classroom is essential. In this regard it is also important to be able to assess the individual aspects of technology that an instructor has chosen to integrate into the classroom, evaluating not only how the teacher plans to apply the content, but how learners will utilize it, and for what pedagogical goals. To this end a 'needs audit' (Bax, 2011) could be conducted first, to assess and evaluate the value of utilizing technology in a particular setting; in other words, determining if technology use is the best method to employ as opposed to another approach that might better lead to the same learning outcomes. This is materials evaluation, something long recognized as important for instructors to consider (Nunan, 1996).

Another long-relied upon method for the analysis and evaluation of technological content has been the checklist (Moncada & Diaz, 2016). The aim of using checklists, and developing technology assessment rubrics, is to lead teachers to a place where they are pedagogically prepared and practically able to implement and evaluate technological content instinctively (see Appendix A for evaluation criteria and rubrics useful when assessing any learning technology.) This can be undertaken by developing criteria that seek to examine the teacher- and student-fit of the technology that is being evaluated to the language theory, methodologies, and approaches that the teacher intends to employ. Particularly if those that are developed are based on appropriate constructs, that can be easily tailored by instructors for their own teaching and learning contexts, and used as a resource that can be applied during pre-, while- and post-implementation evaluation.

This has led to the development of a conceptual model (see Table A1) and the development of a technology integration evaluation rubric (TIER; see Table A2), which can be adapted to specific teaching and learning environments in order to analyze and evaluate the applicability and usability of different technologies for digital language learning and teaching. Accompanying this is a blank template that you can utilize to create an individualized rubric for your own purposes (see Table A3). The five core constructs and criteria behind the TIER, are those of:
1. technology (purpose, teacher-fit, student-fit),
2. content (accuracy, currency, adaptability),
3. reflection (professional development, assessment suitability),
4. usability (significance, adds-value, usefulness, uniqueness, deployment), and
5. resources (existing content).

Core Construct One
When thinking about technology we need to consider its purpose, if it aligns with our learning objectives and provide content that can lead to learning, and if it can be used in a way that fits us as teachers and our learners as students.

Core Construct Two
When thinking about content we need to consider accuracy, authenticity, currency, and adaptability, to determine if the information is accurate, up-to-date, used in real-world contexts, and if it can be tailored to our learning content, reused, and shared.

Core Construct Three
When reflecting upon the effectiveness of the technology we use, we should look at it from both our perspective as a teacher as well as from the student perspective, and very often the teacher perspective is neglected. So, think about how the technology helps you improve as a teacher. Does it offer professional development opportunities? *or* Is it useful for improving upon your existing teacher toolkit? For students, does it provide a range of access and activity options, and the ability to resubmit or redo work if necessary?

Core Construct Four
Usability of technology needs considering in terms of how its use is important, adds value, contributes to the classroom and learning, and how it could be best utilized to maximize instructor time with students by providing them with quality tailored digital language learning opportunities.

Core Construct Five
Finally, when looking at using technology with learners you should be on the lookout for existing resources, content already developed by teachers, so that you don't have to reinvent the wheel. If there is not a good community of content then the potential exists to start creating one, and that then ties back to the professional development component mentioned earlier under the reflection considerations (core construct three).
Materials evaluation has long been recognized as important (Nunan, 1996), with the method and format of the evaluation also important to consider, particularly for those instructors, and pre-service teachers, still honing technological evaluation skills, because this is not something that is innate, and something that Moncada and Diaz (2016) suggest comes with the development of background knowledge and from practice utilizing checklists.

The use or development of a checklist, is advantageous as is it can be explicit, convenient, cost effective, and systematic, although they can sometimes also be very subjective (Lee, 2012). However, if developed based on appropriate core constructs, like those above, they can be easily tailored by instructors for their own teaching and learning context, and during pre-, while- and post-implementation evaluations. So, instructors really do need to think about use carefully, and not just grab anything and go with it to see if it works. In this regard, Levy and Stockwell (2006, p. 46) suggest that language instructors need to be "third-party evaluators" and responsible for making judgments of the overall appropriateness and quality of digital content based on their unique teaching approach, the curriculum being implemented, the learning context, and student needs. Taking these perspectives into account in order to evaluate and assess how we apply technology helps us to explore the rationale and benefits of engaging students with various learning opportunities, and how we might as instructors begin to best implement and integrate them into our classrooms from a question-based perspective.

Teaching in the Time of Digital Language Learning

A question-based approach to analysis and evaluation of learning technologies is important. Since the rise of the fourth industrial revolution, educators have needed to rethink the goals, applicability, use cases, and the integration of technology into the classroom. Instructors need to begin to integrate technology in a way that allows its use to significantly redefine the learning space for students, and themselves as teachers, by replacing traditional teaching methods or learner interactions with alternates that add value. What is required, then, is a model that helps teachers to easily understand the usefulness of different applications, websites, or digital tasks when reviewing them for use with students, and to understand and perhaps rethink how those

Teaching in the Time of Digital Language Learning | 15

activities can uniquely capitalize on providing learning within specific educational contexts, and if they are in fact worthwhile to implement at all. This is important because teaching in the time of digital language learning sees us not just doing old things in new ways, but it has ushered in an era of 'newness'. There are new things to do, new ways to think, new methods of managing relationships with others (and AI), and new practices in teaching that require us to adapt new skills and new abilities (Jones & Hafner, 2012). Ultimately then, when considering technological choices for your learning and teaching context, keep the following question-based approach in mind:

1. What is/are …?
2. How can I use …?
3. What types of … exist?
4. What elements are behind an effective …?
5. How can … lend itself to TESOL?
6. How can I start using … with students?
7. How do I evaluate …?
8. What tools are available for … creation?
9. How do I craft …?
10. How would I use a tool to create …?

To understand this approach perhaps take the TIE (technology integration evaluation) challenge (see Appendix B) as you read through the following points (1 through 10)

1. Determine how the technology that you are considering is *significant*, and how it can be used to enhance specific learning outcomes in a way that is better than the traditional or existing methods that you use. For example, digital assistants can go one step beyond dictionaries as they provide definitions, spellings, and translations while allowing students to practice speaking and listening to

find out these answers, and reading and writing skills if submitting those answers for homework or in an activity completion. Further significance of a digital assistant is that it can provide support for tasks and classroom management while also delivering opportunities for voice-driven learning for students. Also, for learners both in and outside of the classroom, these devices have the potential to provide one-on-one individualized support for engaging in language learning and language practice.
2. Think about how using the technology you are considering *adds value*. For example, if it improves on past experiences by providing a means of distributing content more easily, like providing copies of handouts or homework via Google Drive, or if it takes the technology out of the hands of students entirely, as is the case with Plickers where everything can be done with the teacher's phone and paper-based handouts.
3. For any given technology, understand what specific aspects of it are *useful* to apply. For example, if the technology provides different quiz types, games, assessment methods, or if it can be used for revision of content or for completing homework, or for the practice of a specific skill. The Socrative application may be one example that could fit several of these uses.
4. Ensure that the technology provides a more *unique* means of content delivery, and is not just the use of technology for its own sake. For example, it might provide a new way of taking a poll in class over hand raising, with anonymity and instant results displayable to all students simultaneously. This is the case of Plickers with the use of QR codes to collect responses and then seeing these responses displayed on the teacher's phone and on a website for all students to see.

5. *Adapt* the technology to cater specifically to your EFL or ESL learning environment. For example, use video editors like WeVideo to create a multimedia digital story, use projectors to display a cloze-exercise, or use an application like Zipgrade to grade student submissions.
6. Determine deployment approaches that *provide learning content* through the technology. For example, select a mode-of-delivery that best suits the technology: teacher- or learner-focused, inside or outside of class use, or for formative assessment purposes, which an application like Plickers would be compatible.
7. Continually *assess the effectiveness* of the technology as part of your teaching toolkit. For example, use pre-fabricated rubrics, or alternatively develop your own (see Table A3).
8. Review existing content, and learn how to *develop* it. For example, understand how to create your own content for use with the technology using learning technologies like Story Speaker to create a choose-your-own adventure story for use with a digital assistant.
9. *Adapt and tailor* the learning content provided through the technology. For example, develop a best-model example that other instructors can modify to be fit for their purpose, then screencast or blog about it.
10. *Understand* the technology well enough to be able to inform colleagues on how to employ it for themselves. For example, develop a walk-through, then present this at a local teacher conference, or share it online through your personal learning environment (such as the TESOL-MALL Facebook group, 2019).

In closing, the most valuable skills that we can offer both ourselves and our students today are those of knowing how to learn, unlearn, and relearn (Toffler, 1970) – liquid skills that are adaptable and can lead to life-long learning opportunities. All of us today must have the skills to implement, manage, and work with new technologies, and to be adaptable problem-solvers who are able to both communicate effectively and are able to work with others in creative ways. As we move forward, we will succeed by working alongside our machines and technology, programming them, rather than being programmed by them, and rather than trying to compete with them, welcoming them into our classrooms and into our learners' lives in ways where they can serve to enhance learning experiences by providing increasingly collaborative, meaningful, multimodal, personalized, and non-linear learning pathways.

Are you ready?

References

Bax, S. (2011). Normalization revisited: The effective use of technology in language education. *International Journal of Computer-Assisted Language Learning and Teaching, 1*(2), 1-15.

Bray, B., & McClasky, K. (2019). Personalize learning: Transform learning for all learners. Retrieved from http://www.personalizelearning.com/2015/11/choice-is-more-than-menu-of-options.html

Carrier, M. (2017). Introduction to digital learning. In M. Carrier, R. Damerow, & K. Bailey (Eds.), *Digital language learning and teaching: Research, theory, and practice* (1-10). New York: Routledge, TIRF.

Carrier, M., and Nye, A. (2016). Empowering teachers for the digital future: What do 21st century teachers need? IATEFL workshop. Retrieved from https://www.youtube.com/watch?v=edUEwqoaP_4

Compleat Lexical Tutor (2019). Compleat Lexical Tutor (v.8.3). Retrieved from https://www.lextutor.ca

Davis, F., Bagozzi, R., & Warshaw, P. (1989). User acceptance of computer technology: a comparison of two theoretical models. *Management Science, 35*(8), 982-1003, https://doi.org.10.1287/mnsc.35.8.982

Doucet, A., Evers, J., Guerra E., Lopez, N., Soskil, M., & Timmers, K. (2018). *Teaching in the Fourth Industrial Revolution: Standing at the precipice*. USA: Routledge.

Fotos, S., & Brown, C. (2004). *New perspectives on CALL for second and foreign language classrooms*. Mahwah, NJ: Lawrence Erlbaum Associates.

Gee, J. P. (2004). *Situated language and learning: A critique of traditional schooling*. New York, NY: Routledge.

Goh, C. C. M. (2015, December). *Professional development for teachers of 21st century English language learners*. Paper presented at the 2015 TESOL Regional Conference: Excellence in Language Instruction: Supporting Classroom Teaching & Learning, Singapore.

Jones, R., & Hafner, C. (2012). *Understanding digital literacies: A practical introduction*. USA: Routledge.

Hamilton, E., Rosenberg, J., & Akcaoglu, M. (2016). The substitution augmentation modification redefinition (SAMR) model: A critical review and suggestions for its use. *TechTrends: Linking Research and Practice to Improve Learning, 60*(5), 433-441.

Kent, D. (2015). Tech: iPadagogy. *The English Connection, 19*(1), 27-30.

Kent, D. (2019). Digital assistants: TESOL strategy guide. Sydney, Australia: Pedagogy Press.

Keskin, N., & Metcalf, D. (2011). The current perspectives, theories and practices of mobile learning. *TOJET: The Turkish Online Journal of Educational Technology, 10*(2), 202-208.

Lee, C. (2015). *Principles and applications of MALL*. Seoul: Bookorea.

Lee, S. (2012). Evaluation of English learning programs on EBSe. In C. Lee (Ed.), *The Handbook of Multimedia-Assisted Language Learning: Theories and Practices* (1068-1083). South Korea: KAMALL.

Levy, M., & Stockwell, G. (2006). Evaluation. In M. Levy & G. Stockwell (Eds.), *CALL dimensions: Options and Issues in Computer-Assisted Language Learning* (pp. 40-83). Mahwah, NJ: Lawrence Erlbaum Associates.

MIT. (2016). Office of digital learning. Retrieved from https://odl.mit.edu/value-digital-learning

Naismith, L., Lonsdale, P., Vavoula, G., & Sharples, M. (2004). *Report 11: Literature review in mobile technologies and learning. Futurelab series.* Bristol, UK: Futurelab.

Nunan, D. (1996). *Learner-centered curriculum.* Cambridge: Cambridge University Press.

Puentedura, R. (2006). Transformation, technology, and education. Retrieved from http://hippasus.com/resources/tte

Richards, J. (2015). The changing face of language learning: Learning beyond the classroom. *RELC, 46*(1), 5-22, https://doi.org/10/1177/00336882145621

Siemens, G. (2005). Connectivism: A learning theory for the digital age. *International Journal of instructional Technology & Distance Learning, 2,* 3-10.

TESOL-MALL Facebook Group. (2019). *TESOL-MALL Graduate Program, Woosong University. 우송대 TESOL 학과.* Retrieved from https://www.facebook.com/groups/889904227718128

Toffler, A. (1970). *Future Shock.* United States: Random House.

Warschauer, M. (2000). The changing global economy and the future of English teaching. *TESOL Quarterly, 34*(3), 511-535.

Wheeler, S. (2013, March 28). Technology won't replace teachers, but … Learning with 'e's. [Blog post]. Retrieved from http://www.steve-wheeler.co.uk/2013/03/technology-wont-replace-teachers-but.html

Appendix A
The TIER (Technology Integration Evaluation Rubric)

The Conceptual Model

Table A1. *The TIER conceptual model*

The Technology Integration Evaluation Rubric Conceptual Model			
Construct	**Criteria**	**Item**	**Example**
Technology	Purpose	Is the app/site purpose clear?	Aligns with learning objectives presented in activities.
		Is the content in line with the purpose?	Content provides learning (e.g., communicative-based).
	Teacher-fit	Is the app/site compatible with your teaching style?	Matches the style of the teacher implementing the content.
	Student-fit	Is the app/site appropriate for use with the target learners?	Matches the style of the learners.

Content	Accuracy	Is the information correct?	No spelling or grammar errors.
	Authenticity	Is the data authentic?	Content comes from real-world data, and is used in real-world contexts.
	Currency	Is the information up-to-date or timeless?	Topics and information from the last five years.
	Adaptability	Can the technology (or the content that it offers) be tailored to learning?	Applicability (can add content on demand; can rework content to a lesson; can utilize it to complete objectives/projects).
		Can the content be reused?	Suitable across different classes and students in the teaching and learning context; can be designed or modified once and then used across classes/students.
		Can the content be shared?	Means to distribute content to all students, between students, to other stakeholders (including Student's output); or the content is locked to a single student/class.

Reflection	Professional development	Can instructor use of the app/site be assessed?	Useful for action research, improving teaching skills.
		Am I able to teach others how to employ this effectively?	Develop a walkthrough.
	Assessment suitability	Can the app/site be used for formative/summative assessment?	Provides a range of assessment choices for learners/instructors (e.g. poll, multiple-choice).
		Can grades be reviewed/resubmitted?	Allows students to redo work and resubmit before final grading.
Usability	Significance	How is the technology important?	Shifts learning (e.g., provides multi-modal learning; meets set standards; provides completion of competency pathways).
	Adds value	How is using the technology adding value?	Improves on past experience (e.g., easier distribution or revision of content).
	Usefulness	How is the technology useful to apply?	Means of use (e.g., provides formative/summative assessment; can be utilized for revision, homework, or skills targeting).

	Uniqueness	How is the technology providing something special?	Provides something old in a new or unique manner (e.g., polls students with anonymity with instant results).
	Deployment	How is the technology best utilized?	Context of use (e.g., in- or out-of-class, individual- pair- or group-work; smartphone, website, printouts).
Resources	*Existing content*	Does teacher-developed content already exist?	Community of content (e.g., a range of resources exists that can be adapted or used as-is to meet current needs, and a place is provided for you to add your content).
Format	*Checklist*	What scale or means will be used for rating the applicability/value of items?	Likert scale (e.g., questions can be scored from 1 to 5 to get a total percentage out of 100 for the technology).

The TIER

Table A2. *The technology integration evaluation rubric*

The Technology Integration Evaluation Rubric		
Aspect	**Criteria**	**Score**
The Technology (hardware or software)	Matches with core learning objectives (e.g., developing fluency, increasing listening practice, practicing vocabulary)	1 2 3 4 5
	Content assists with learner development (e.g., provides communicative fluency, grammar-based activities)	1 2 3 4 5
	Meshes well with the instructor (e.g., teaching style, classroom management techniques, time for development and incorporation into lesson plans)	1 2 3 4 5
	Appropriate for use with the target learner (e.g., age, language level, motivation)	1 2 3 4 5
Content	Content and software is error-free (e.g., no bugs; no spelling, grammar, or pronunciation errors)	1 2 3 4 5
	Provides relevant content and topics (e.g., authentic, timeless, up-to-date, holistically useful)	1 2 3 4 5
	Content can be modified, tailored, or guided for effective use (e.g., add content on demand, rework content to a lesson)	1 2 3 4 5
	Content is reusable (e.g., with the same students, across classes, across the curriculum)	1 2 3 4 5

	Content is shareable (e.g., not locked to a single student/class, distributable to other stakeholders)	1 2 3 4 5
Reflection	Instructor use of the technology provides growth (e.g., leads to action research, pedagogical improvement)	1 2 3 4 5
	Easy to teach others how to apply the technology (e.g., develop a walkthrough)	1 2 3 4 5
	Variable assessment types (e.g., poll or multiple-choice for either formative or summative use)	1 2 3 4 5
	Reviewability (e.g., if assessable: grades can be seen and reviewed; work can be resubmitted by students)	1 2 3 4 5
Usability	Provides a learning shift (e.g., creates multi-modal learning, meets set standards; provides completion of competency pathways)	1 2 3 4 5
	Improves on past learning experiences (e.g., easier distribution or revision of content)	1 2 3 4 5
	Usefulness (e.g., provides formative/summative assessment; can be utilized for revision, homework, skills targeting)	1 2 3 4 5
	Distinctive, provides something old in a new way (e.g., polls students instantly with anonymity)	1 2 3 4 5

	Suitable for	in-class work	1 2 3 4 5
		out-of-class work	1 2 3 4 5
		individual work	1 2 3 4 5
		pair work	1 2 3 4 5
		group work	1 2 3 4 5
		use with accompanying handouts	1 2 3 4 5
		use alongside other technologies (phone/website/etc.)	1 2 3 4 5
Resources	Community of content (e.g., a range of resources exist that can be adapted or used as-is)		1 2 3 4 5
Score	Obtain a total across all aspects to compare between various application types, websites, or other digital language learning technologies		_____
	Ratings: 1 Poor 2 Fair 3 Average 4 Good 5 Excellent		

The TIER Template

It can be useful to rely on a template to help you think about the rationale behind the development of your own analysis and evaluation of website or application use in the classroom, and as a means of identifying those aspects of technology integration that are weak and those that align well with target objectives. In order to help you in this process, an example of a template in development and a blank template to complete, along with definitions and examples for each of the terms presented in the template, are provided here.

Template term definitions

Construct is the major overall aspect that you are looking to evaluate. For example, content.

Criteria breaks down the construct (overall aspect) into smaller components that you want to focus upon during your evaluation. For example, accuracy.

Item is what you are specifically looking to ensure that the website or application does (this can be a statement or a question). For example, it provides information that is correct.

Example is one thing that your item would be able to confirm. This will help you pinpoint the kind of thing you are specifically looking for in response to the item. For example, no spelling or grammar errors.

Format is the method of providing a score or overall analysis/evaluation synthesis. You can enter this decision in the final row of the table as shown in the example. Here, each item is rated 1 to 5 to get a total obtain an overall score.

Table A3. *The TIER template*

The Technology Integration Evaluation Rubric Template			
Construct	**Criteria**	**Item**	**Example**
Format			

Complete the template sections as required,
adding or deleting rows as appropriate.

Appendix B
The TIE (Technology Integration Evaluation) Challenge

For an item of technology that you currently use in the classroom how does it fit each of the key points for considering technological choices in the time of digital language learning and teaching.

Table B1. *The TIE challenge*

Technology (app/website/etc.)	
Significance	
Value-added	
Usefulness	
Uniqueness	
Adaptability	
Deployment Method(s)	
Effective Assessment	
Development Options	
Tailorability	
Professional Development Options	

How does your use of technology match up?

2. Chatbots as Conversational Agents in the Context of Language Learning

Daniel Bailey
Konkuk University Glocal Campus

Introduction

A conversational agent is a concept borrowed from computer science and artificial intelligence and applied to education as part of an intelligent tutoring system. Conversational agents are simulated human-like interfaces that use voice, images, text, and more to engage students naturally through language. The term *conversational agent* was chosen to describe the automatic online messaging applications in this chapter, but other terms like *pedagogical agent*, *chatbot*, and *virtual assistant* have also been used to describe similar online messaging programs. Voice communication programs like conversational agents can be used to increase learner participation (i.e., task engagement) and learning outcomes (D'Mello & Sidney, 2008; Procter, Lin, & Heller, 2012; Shum, He, & Li, 2018; Szafir & Mutlu, 2012). This chapter posits that chatbots can be used as conversational agents that help students overcome writing challenges by providing an opportunity for L2 (second language) writing practice through interactive roleplay, storytelling, and simulated text messaging.

Conversational agents

Conversational agents (CAs) can use natural language (i.e., a language developed naturally in use) to assist in writing strategy instruction, idea-generation, goal setting, and reflection. Through messaging, students can communicate with the CA about daily activities, personal goals, favorites (places, food, people, and games), and relationships. Each conversational agent interaction should bring value to the student. Here is a list of some things that CAs can do: engage students through storytelling, describe activities, persuade students to write, archive student-CA interactions, answer frequently asked questions (assignment criteria and due dates), get help from a live-support instructor, entertain students (e.g., jokes, videos, music, images), reengage low participating students, remind students about incomplete assignments, and deliver class news.

Conversational agents are currently being used for product and service marketing purposes. Small and large companies are employing CAs as social media marketing tools because they are relatively simple to create and result in higher interaction rates with consumers than other forms of online marketing (e.g., email and website advertisements). Conversational agents can be used as an interaction layer between learning activities and students, just as businesses use them as interaction layers between brands and consumers. For marketing, these messengers are designed to complement the website and social media presence using scripted conversations with potential customers.

Research is currently exploring methods to produce better CAs by making them more social (Shum, He, & Li, 2018). Following the Perceptions-Actions Hypothesis, CAs programmed with natural language that includes emotion and empathy are expected to promote stronger relationships and collaboration (Davis, 1994; de Waal, 2010; Hoffman, 2001), and this results in more learner-CA interactions with more words per interaction. Shum, He, and Li (2018) recognize that adding empathy and emotional utterances in conversational agent communication produced complex interactions. CAs are pedagogical agents that model positive behavior (e.g., task-interest, engagement, motivation) towards a task.

In addition to pedagogically goal-driven communication, CAs use phatic talk (e.g., small talk) and persuasive language to motivate students to engage in learning activities. A phatic expression serves social functions such as social pleasantries and conversation for the sake of conversation. Persuasive writing through CA interactions can use phatic expressions to appeal to students' emotions and empathy. Persuasive writing can also use language to convince readers to believe in an idea and engage in an action. CAs use persuasive writing to motivate students to engage in learning tasks. A task goal with CAs is to convince students to participate in learning activities by appealing to their emotions, reasoning, and logic. Persuasive writing is common in advertising where marketing professionals try to convince consumers to buy a product or service, and these same marketing techniques that are used for brand-awareness can be used for task-awareness in education.

Conversational agents use natural language networks to allow complex communication with users through conversation dialogues (Hold, Dubs, Jones, & Greer, 1994). A conversation dialogue is a graphical model that represents a set of variables and their conditional dependencies (Gal, 2007). Each node in the conversation dialogue is associated with a particular set of values for the branch's parent variables and gives subsequent options for students to select which are represented by the node. CA responses are based on user inputs, and those that are close-ended (button input options) decrease the risk of miscommunication between the user and CA. Interactions between CAs and learners through a series of statements provided by CAs and responses chosen by students is central to research in intelligent tutoring systems (Michaud & McCoy, 2006; Zapata-Rivera & Greer, 2004; Reye, 2004). A key to successful communication is having a purpose behind each interaction. For instance, the CA should be only meant to communicate with the user, or in other words, student, for a few minutes about a specific topic. When the topic is something like food, the content delivered only needs to be about food. The conversational agent controls the narrative of the conversation through storytelling, leading questions, and close-ended responses.

The use of automated conversation-dialogue trees has been popular in video games and interactive novels for many years. An example of a conversation may begin by the CA stating, 'Hi, [name]. How are you doing today?' and this can be responded to in a variety of ways depending on how the dialogue tree is programmed (e.g., *I'm doing well, Not so good,* or *I'm busy right now*). The CA then responds depending on how the student answered (e.g., *Fantastic, Do you have time to chat?, That's too bad,* or *Maybe I can help cheer you up*).

The complexity of the conversation dialogue trees depends on the chatbot designers' programming skills. Teachers without programming knowledge who are interested in building conversational agents should visit platforms like Chatfuel (www.chatfuel.com) or Manychat (www.manychat.com) while computer savvy teachers can explore the capabilities of Google's Dialogflow (www.dialogflow.com), or even Heruko (www.heruko.com). There are ample tutorials for all of these platforms on sites like YouTube and Udemy (www.udemy.com).

Kerly, Hall, & Bull (2007) investigated a CA system that allowed people to negotiate meaning when using natural language, and their study explored the feasibility of integrating a CA into an open learner model system to enable student-system negotiation over the contents of the learner model. They investigated the feasibility of using a CA to support learning activities, and in their study, as a precursor to the development of a CA, they used a Wizard-of-Oz method to conduct an experiment where the role of the CA was taken by the experimenter: the Wizard. The user (or student) did not know that the CA was not a human until after the study to ensure that data collected from their interaction would be pertinent to human-computer conversational design. The most common questions that CAs helped students with were related to activity instructions, help with activities, direction on what needed to be studied, and clarification with misconceptions. Kerly et al. (2007) recommend that CAs provide links to relevant databases and websites. Furthermore, CAs should follow common user requests and keep the user on topic.

CA programs display behavior that users will interpret as understanding through extensive syntactic structures developed for natural language processing and complex methodological data structuring. Kerly et al. (2007) found that students held positive perceptions toward CAs, and the researchers recommend that future studies explore using CAs to provide details about courses, assignments, and training through which students are able to demonstrate their knowledge and skills.

Conversational agents employ gamification elements to increase student participation. Gamification is described as "using game-based mechanics, aesthetics, and game thinking to engage people, motivate action, and promote learning" (Kapp, 2012, p. 10). Perry (2015) investigated the use of an augmented reality videogame to help students learn French where students experienced roleplay adventures through close-ended choices (i.e., dialogue trees). The findings indicate that students were motivated by gamification mechanics like collecting badges and collaborating with classmates. Furthermore, students enjoyed practicing L2 vocabulary outside of class within an immersive language learning environment. Alias et al. (2014) sought to better understand how professional language educators perceive narrative-based roleplay video games, and survey analysis of 30 experts found that augmented reality games and mobile learning will dominate trends in the future. These experts strongly agreed that video games are especially beneficial for L2 vocabulary acquisition, but these simple benefits are a major limitation to our current understanding of how mobile-learning roleplay activities influence language learning because these activities are quite time-consuming.

There are a number of limitations with using CAs in education. Thompson, Gallacher, and Howarth (2018) examined the impact of CAs as conversation partners, and their data suggested that

Chatbots as Conversational Agents | 37

students found the messenger responses inappropriate and the interaction as being unnatural. To mitigate miscommunications between CAs and users, instructors who wish to use CAs should use a combination of close-ended responses (e.g., button replies) and guiding questions. The service industry uses the same technique when asking customers or prospects to interact with their company chatbot. An example of a simple dialogflow diagram that follows this path is shown in Figure 1.

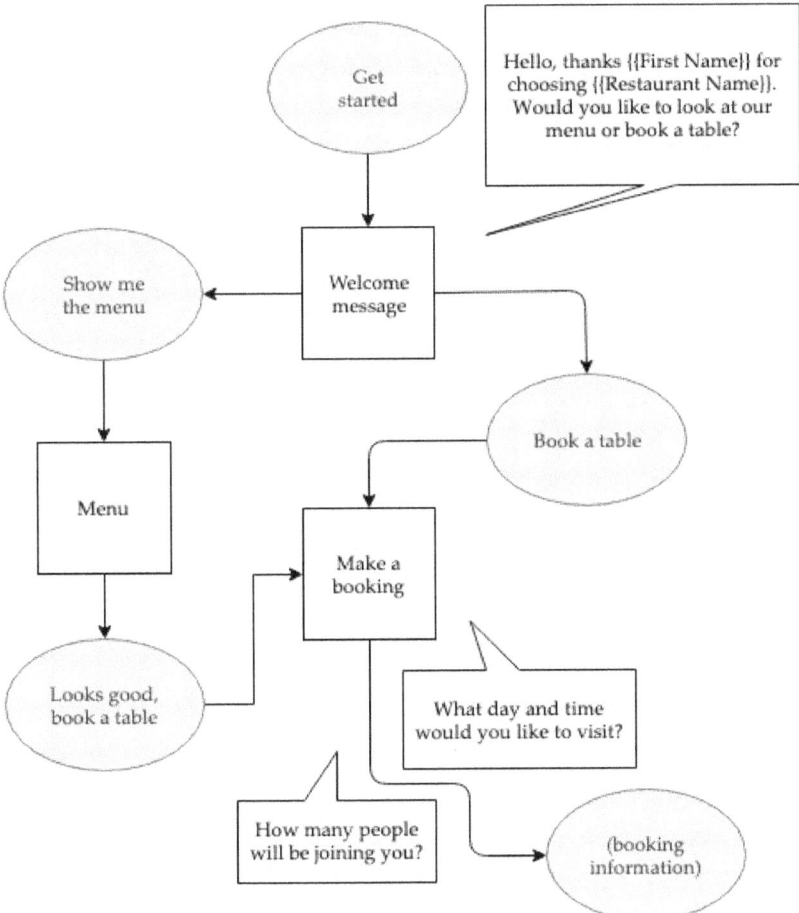

Figure 1. Simple dialog flow for a restaurant reservation chatbot

In the restaurant example, the user is asked a series of questions which can be answered using a combination of close-ended button responses and open-ended short text responses. The answers can either be sent to a database for storage or entered into a conditional program (e.g., if user says X then CA replies with Y). Figure 2 shows how the same CA design approach that is used for restaurant reservation scenarios can be used with conversational agents in the EFL context. Instead of asking about a product or service, the CA models language use by telling a short story and then asks leading questions to the student to elicit content which is then sent to a storage site like Google Sheets. Platforms like Chatfuel, Manychat, and others are designed for non-developers who want to build chatbots for their companies or as hobbies. These platforms are ideal for low tech-savvy teachers.

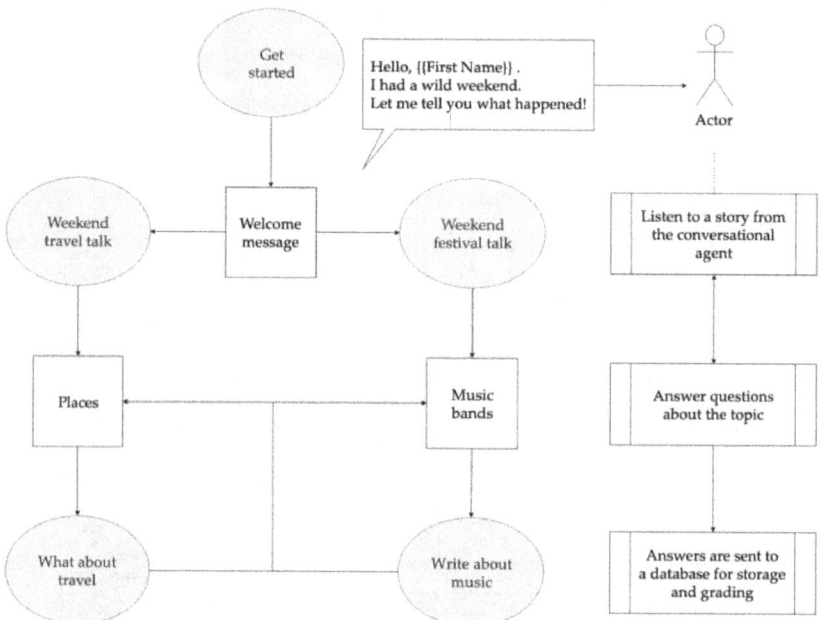

Figure 2. Simple dialog flow for an EFL conversational agent designed for providing writing practice

Conversational agent technology continues to improve in quality and decrease in cost. There is now a need to understand how CA communication can be used to increase interest, task-value, and self-efficacy in learning environments. Increased writing practice from CA engagement may have a number of pedagogical implications that future studies should investigate. For instance, there is a need to research the effect conversational agents have on L2 writing accuracy, complexity, and fluency. L2 writing anxiety is expected to be lower when communicating with a conversational agent because, after all, the CA is just a machine. Therefore, future research should investigate the possible effect that CAs have on L2 writing anxiety. This chapter discusses the mode of communication with conversational agents through the lens of text messaging. The same research designs that are carried out with text-messaging can be duplicated in the context of voice communication. Spoken interactions with conversational agents would have potential benefits to pronunciation and fluency that would be worth exploring. While there is a healthy body of literature on the application of conversational agents in L1 (first language) education, there is a drastic lack of research that examines conversational agents as tools for L2 acquisition.

References

Alias, N., Rosman, F., Rahman, M. N. A., & Dewitt, D. (2015). The potential of video game in Malay language learning for foreign students in a public higher education institution. *Procedia – Social and Behavioral Sciences, 176*, 1020-1027.

Davis, M. H. (1994). *Empathy: A social psychological approach.* USA: Westview Press.

De Waal, F. B. M. (2010). *The age of empathy: nature's lessons for a kinder society.* USA: Three Rivers Press.

D'Mello, S. K., & Craig, S. D. (2008). Automatic detection of learner's affect from conversational cues. *User Modeling User-Adapted Interaction*, 18(1-2), 45-80, https://doi.org/10.1007/s11257-007-9037-6

Gal, B. I. (2007). "Bayesian Networks". In F. Ruggeri, R. Kennett, and F. Faltin. *Encyclopedia of Statistics in Quality and Reliability*. USA: John Wiley & Sons. https://doi:10.1002/9780470061572.eqr089

Hoffman, M. L. (2001). *Empathy and moral development: Implications for caring and justice*. Cambridge: Cambridge University Press.

Kapp, K. (2012). *The gamification of learning and instruction: Game-based methods and strategies for training and education*. USA: John Wiley & Sons.

Kerly, A., Hall, P., & Bull, S. (2007). Bringing bots into education: Towards natural language negotiation of open learner models, in R. Ellis, T. Allen, & A. Tuson (Eds), Applications and innovations in intelligent Systems XIV – *Proceedings of AI-2006, 26th SGAI International Conference on Innovative Techniques and Applications of Artificial Intelligence*, Springer, https://doi.org/10.1007/978-1-84628-666-7

Michaud, L. N., & McCoy, K. F. (2006). Capturing the evolution of grammatical knowledge in a CALL system for deaf learners of English. *International Journal of Artificial Intelligence in Education*, 16(1), 65-97.

Perry, B. (2015). Gamifying French language learning: A case study examining a quest-based, augmented reality mobile learning-tool. *Procedia – Social and Behavioral Sciences*, 174, 2308-2315.

Procter, M., Lin, F., & Heller, B. (2012). Intelligent intervention by conversational agent through chatlog analysis. *Smart Learning Environments*, 5(30), 1-15.

Szafir, D., and Mutlu, B. (2012). Pay attention!: Designing adaptive agents that monitor and improve user engagement. In J. Konstan, and E. Chi (Eds.), *Proceedings of the SIGCHI Conference on Human Factors in Computing Systems* (pp. 11-20). Austin, Texas, USA. https://10.1145/2207676.2207679

Thompson, A., Gallacher, A., & Howarth, M. (2018). Stimulating task interest: human partners or chatbots? *Future-proof CALL: Language learning as exploration and encounters – short papers from EUROCALL 2018,* 302-306.

Reye, J. (2004). Student modelling based on belief networks. *International Journal of Artificial Intelligence in Education, 14*(1), 63-96.

Shum, H.-Y., He, X., & Li. D. (2018). From Eliza to XiaoIce: Challenges and opportunities with social chatbots. *Frontiers of Information Technology & Electronic Engineering, 19*(1), 10-16. https://doi.org/10.1631/FITEE.1700826

Wang, J. L., Jackson, L. A., Wang, H. Z., & Gaskin, J. (2015). Predicting social networking site (SNS) use: Personality, attitudes, motivation and internet self-efficacy. *Personality and Individual Differences, 80*(1), 119-124.

Zapata-Rivera, J. D., & Greer, J. E. (2004). Interacting with inspectable Bayesian student models. *International Journal of Artificial Intelligence in Education, 14*(2), 127-163.

Zhang, L. J., Qin, T. L. (2018). Validating a questionnaire on EFL writers' metacognitive awareness of writing strategies in multimedia environment. In A. Haukas, & M. Dypedahl (Eds.), *Metacognition in Language Learning and Teaching* (pp. 157-177). London, England: Routledge (Taylor & Francis Group).

3. Practical and Innovative Applications for Wikis in a Language Classroom

Michael Cary
Kyonggi University – Main Campus, Suwon

The Beginning*

In the forward of the seminal book on wikis (Leuf & Cunningham, 2005), Ron Jeffries writes about how Ward Cunningham (his teacher and the creator of the first wiki) asked, "What would you get if you had a Web site where anyone could edit or add anything?" He had posited that boredom or chaos would ensue, and states, "Boy, was I wrong" (p. xiii). Keeping this in mind, any discussion of wikis then must first mention the world-renowned site Wikipedia, which as Richardson (2009) and Miller (2004) state, has a goal of being the "sum of all human knowledge" (¶ 2). While every bit of human knowledge may not yet be on Wikipedia, more pages are constantly accepted and added regularly so this goal may one day be realized.

Wikipedia

Ward Cunningham, the inventor of wikis, first created WikiWikiWeb in 1994 and released it in 1995 (Richardson, 2009) which was the real beginning for wikis. Wikipedia was then released and went live January 15, 2001 with the help of Jimmy Wales and Larry Sanger who built on Cunningham's wiki concept (Wikipedia contributors, 2019a). With this new Web 2.0 technology, wikis burst onto the online stage and were viewed as controversial in the educational community because Wikipedia seemed to increase the ease of plagiarizing, with a general view of it as suspicious, as

---

Note: The author wishes to thank Chris Slycord and Carlo Gentile for assisting in the development of this chapter.

Practical and Innovative Applications for Wikis | 43

> Teachers in middle school, high school and college drill it in to their students: Wikipedia is not a citable source. Anyone can edit Wikipedia, and articles can change from day to day – sometimes by as little as a comma, other times being completely rewritten overnight. (Brookshire, 2018, ¶ 2).

Due to this, teachers may be reluctant to assign major writing tasks to students of ESL and EFL for fear of just receiving 'copy pasta' or a paper written mostly from copying and pasting things from Wikipedia. I assure you that not all wikis or the use of even your own wiki need to have anything to do with Wikipedia or using the creation options available on Wikipedia.

Wikipedia is ranked as the fifth top website, third if removing search engines (Alexa Internet Inc., 2019), and several books have been written about it that highlight its importance (Ayers, Matthews, Yates, 2008; Dalby, 2009; Skiena & Ward, 2013). So, what are wikis, then? "Wikis are collaborative web-based environments that allow multiple users to easily and quickly contribute content," (Matthew, Felvegi, & Callaway, 2009, p. 51). A wiki is simply a type of website that anyone can make and each can range from completely free to having monthly or yearly fees to maintain them. A multitude of wikis have been created to date and cover nearly every field known to man (Wikipedia contributors, 2019b). Industry and teaching can use wikis to enhance many various aspects of learning (Richardson, 2009; Malamed, 2019). Wikis can be completely visible to the public, password protected, have editing options that can be open to any registered user of a particular wiki creation site company (like Wikipedia is), or a wiki can restrict its members. The visibility and editing options can fit whatever needs one could desire. Wikipedia is the most widely known wiki (Alexa Internet Inc., 2019) and it is open to everyone in the world, meaning that anyone with internet access can read, edit, and change its content, as Cunningham (2001) states a wiki is a website that anyone can edit and add things to, but some wikis you might never know exist or who might be editing them (e.g., those run by certain industries or teachers who password protect their wikis and do not disclose the website freely). That said, anyone can create their own unique wiki to fit whatever online needs to connect to the world or to others that they desire.

The Validity of Wikipedia

The Nature article 'Internet encyclopedias go head to head' (Giles, 2005) demonstrated that Wikipedia's level of accuracy approached that of Encyclopedia Britannica, and Time magazine in 2006 stated that Wikipedia is "the biggest and possibly best encyclopedia in the world," (Anderson, 2006, ¶ 1), so any language classroom can find reliably good ways to use Wikipedia to enhance learning, and it is often viewed as a starting point for research into any topic by many people (Brookshire, 2018). Although the use of Wikipedia only as a reading tool is not what wikis are about, and the whole remarkableness of Wikipedia relates to the fact that anyone can choose to add or change the information on it, the point of wikis is that anyone can create and add people to one and start creating content.

Wikipedia and TESOL

The TESOL (Teaching English to speakers of other languages) International Association as an organization has many goals and seeks to enhance the learning and teaching of English around the world (TESOL International Association, 2019). As it has been stated, Wikipedia is attempting to warehouse the sum of all human knowledge, and it is true that there are many topics related to the TESOL Association already on Wikipedia (see Wikipedia contributors, 2019c), and in fact, there is even a KOTESOL (Korea teachers of English to speakers of other languages association) wiki page to be found. Any teacher of English as a foreign or second language can learn useful information from the website, and become a registered user with Wikipedia and begin to help edit and to add content to these pages. It is quite likely that some of you may have already edited information on Wikipedia.

KOTESOL Chapters
In addition to being able to add and change this sum of TESOL knowledge that everyone can easily find and know about, many others of us out there can create wikis to help our own particular teaching areas. That aside, there are many various TESOL associations that exist all over the world including in the Republic of Korea (hereafter Korea). There are currently nine registered KOTESOL chapters in Korea with links already established on the Wikipedia website and you can easily check them out and join Wikipedia if you want to add to this globally recognized source of information related to these chapters. I am sure that almost everyone on the peninsula is only an hour or less away by public transport from one of these main chapter areas (except for those who live on Jeju). If you want more personalized information and resources concerning your area and the TESOL field, a wiki can easily accomplish this and it can be better controlled or managed than perhaps a Facebook group. Wikis also make it possible to create a convenient way to interact with each other on a sharing and professional basis.

A TESOL Community Connected
Wikis may be able to connect different TESOL professionals from all over the world, as Wikipedia has shown since it has over 27 million registered users and pages in twenty different languages (Anderson, Hitlin, & Atkinson, 2016). All that you need to do is create your own wiki and you can connect, reconnect, and collaborate with anyone that you know in the world no matter where they are. While I haven't done any wiki collaborations with classrooms in other countries besides the ones where I have

taught (Korea and the United States of America), other teachers have (Chew & Ding, 2014; Richardson, 2009). It is my goal and hope for the field of TESOL to start connecting our students with various students of other teachers of English around the world. In the future, I hope to set up a shared class environment through a wiki in which my students in Suwon can work together building knowledge between each other and students from a class in Yogyakarta, Indonesia where a fellow TESOL professional I went to school with teaches. I am sure most teachers are aware of others they consider friends and highly skilled professionals who live very far away from them and a wiki can bring you, your students, and your ideas together in a shared space online. Wikis can serve TESOL associations as well, serving all of their members by connecting us, building our knowledge, and creating a new teaching environment that all of us can help lead and build.

Philosophy behind Using Wikis in EFL Classrooms:
Teaching Methodologies

Current language teaching methodologies in TESOL revolve around Vygotsky's (1978) notion of language being a social interaction and needing a Zone of Proximal Development (ZPD). Krashen (1981) built on this idea with the concept of $i + 1$, or that learners should be exposed to language just far enough beyond their current competence so that they can understand most but not all language input to still be challenged in order to make progress in the language. Many teachers in classrooms today also draw heavily upon Gardner's (1983) theory of multiple intelligences to create individualization in a classroom and to allow for students to feel what they are learning is relevant and meaningful to their lives. Due to the tremendous versatility wikis give teachers, they certainly will help create innovative and unique learning environments for our students, which is of course helping to enhance the field of TESOL and learning and teaching in the future (Richardson, 2009; Kent, 2017). Chew and Ding (2014) came to the conclusion that:

> The polarity between the ZPD and the ZDD [Zone of Distal Development] lies not in the functional use of wikis but in the degree of openness and social presence of the participants in Chinese language studies, especially with regard to educational practices and pedagogical changes in the critical peer review process and the discourse regarding the use of wikis (p. 198).

Previous literature also suggests that using a wiki in your class is an excellent tool for constructivist learning principles and working collaboratively (Englstrom & Jewett, 2005; Murugesan, 2007; West & West, 2009). Zokor's (2009) study also suggests that wikis can be used to enhance effective collaboration in a constructivist approach for all types of language learning. It is up to you to be creative and innovative , and perhaps as I have done you will be able to experience joy in your classrooms as long as you can get your students to be comfortable and embrace your ideas (see my wikis for example, Cary, 2019a, 2019b, 2019c).

Pragmatics and TBLT

I think that it is important to consider pragmatics as well. As Herraiz-Martinez (2018) states, "The main concern of language educators is how to develop an accurate pragmatic behavior in instructional settings," (p.42). She also stresses, "the key point is the importance of selecting activities that have clear goals," (p.38). You can use a wiki for simply archiving all of your videos, handouts, schedule for assignments, Microsoft PowerPoint files, and any other classroom resources that you are going to use during a semester or term. Though, if you are going to use a wiki to help aid in your students learning potential as I hope you do, you will need, as Kent (2017) states, to have goals that focus upon what you want your students doing with the wiki. Pragmatics, as Bardovi-Harlig (2013) simply put, is "the study of how-to-say-what-to-whom-when," (p. 68) and in order to accomplish this, many teachers and instructors have adopted a task-based language teaching (TBLT) approach. Herraiz-Martinez (2018) demonstrates that, "the teaching of pragmatics through the use of tasks may lead to maximize the potential of technological innovations for students to engage in doing things" (p. 43).

Further guidance into how to design classes around a TBLT approach is detailed in Willis and Willis (2012) to achieve the desired goal of teaching the language by engaging learners in real language use in the classroom by using tasks. Many teachers are aware of the tasks they do in their classroom that achieve the goal of students producing and understanding real-world practical use of the language, but some may want guidance into the teaching approach that this book illustrates. So, with a little reading and creativity you can find a way to make a wiki and your goals work together.

Goals

Before you go off and start making wiki after wiki though, any wise teacher should think carefully about what their teaching and learning goals are for the class they are teaching. Once you have clearly defined what yours are for the class and your students, then you can better design a wiki to fit your needs. A wiki is a great place for teachers to create a collaborative online learning environment for their students as long as clear goals are defined. For instance, during my MA TESOL program, the professor had us complete a website review assignment. I chose wikis, but I didn't get a very good grade because I wrote that a wiki is the only website that you will ever need as a teacher since wikis are so limitless in their potential. It is certainly true that a wiki can be used to centralize all things that you could use in a class by adding almost anything found online, or materials you have offline, to a wiki even inviting your students to participate in doing so. The reason why I received low marks on that assignment is because I never clearly defined a teaching goal to be met by using a wiki. A teacher must clearly instruct their students about the goals they are trying to achieve in the classroom and how the online components in class will help to achieve these. Otherwise, a teacher will find that students do not understand the purpose of what they are doing (Barjami & Ismaili, 2016).

Further information for creating an effective wiki will be detailed in the following sections but keeping pragmatics and tasked-based assignments in mind should help guide you with your goals. For creating a wiki, there are a limited few creation sites to choose from that are still easy to create nowadays. Usually, it just involves registering a unique name and verifying your wiki through an email account. However, why would one want to create a wiki for teaching in the first place?

Digital Natives
Prensky (2001) coined the term *digital natives* to refer to those who are brought up surrounded by digital technologies, computers, and access to the internet. For such students, even though they may or may not be technologically savvy, the teacher should certainly aim to include the use of technology into the classes that they teach. Indeed, we expect to be incorporating technologies into our teaching now (Kent, 2019), and one way of doing this is to include the use of wikis.

Video and Audio are Necessary in Your Classroom
After conducting needs analyses on classes I have taught and still teach, I have found that a vast majority of my students possess a high interest in language learning from video and audio sources. Bajrami and Ismaili (2016) suggest "that both teachers and students can be involved in creative ways to incorporate different video materials in a variety of classroom activities to enhance learning outcomes and provide a positive classroom environment" (p. 505). You can embed videos into wikis as I will

soon illustrate, and videos can be found on the internet at sites such as TeacherTube, YouTube, and Vimeo. All three of these sites vary in options and features that warrant chapters in themselves on how one can best implement the use of videos in a classroom. There are also various sites such as SoundCloud, BandCamp, Spotify, and other very well known music and/or audio streaming sites that can be embedded into a wiki to help enhance the audio content you cover or want to create or have students create in your classes.

Audacity is a useful free open-source downloadable program that can do audio recording, editing, and saving audio files in various formats that can then be uploaded or embedded within a wiki. It is also possible to record multiple tracks separately and layer them onto a single track (see Appendix A). Video editing software is also useful for teachers to learn in order to use a wiki as effectively as possible since Bajrami and Ismaili (2016) highlight that, "video materials nowadays are not only part of everyday life activities, but they are shown as an effective method in teaching English language as a foreign language for all learners both inside and outside the classroom" (p. 502), and a wide range of free and pay video editing software exists. However, as programs constantly change, adapt, or, sadly, disappear, it is important for teachers to be aware of and be able to use video and audio to create intriguing and diverse classroom activities, and they should stay up-to-date with the various websites and programs for use in their classrooms.

Video Potential

I was able to introduce my students to a farmers' dialog in Jamaican Patois by showing a current reggae song by Max Romeo called The Farmer's Story (2019), one that discusses local farming and corporate enterprise. This fit perfectly with the book unit topic that I was teaching, while demonstrating real use of a dialect that many of the learners in the class have never been exposed to.

The video portal site when playing back the song allowed for the option of displaying lyrics on the screen so that students could better follow the provided handout and it was sung in clear English. This video was an official video, so the portal allowed viewers to change its speed, with the possibility of playing it back as slowly as 25% that of the original speed so that students could better understand it.

It is possible to use so many similar technologies within a wiki for your classes, from YouTube videos to Audacity use and SoundCloud, and it is important that we use technology in our classrooms to effectively teach these digital natives and adapt their learning to fit their future world. By having a wiki, you are able to centralize your resources throughout a semester or term, and depending on how you use it, you can see student learning taking place whether you create a class-wide wiki that they can join or you have them create one for themselves. Every wiki that is created can adapt and change, so it gives a teacher the tremendous benefit of being able to have an adaptable online curriculum that still maintains permanence year after year.

Diversity
Why else should you choose a wiki? Well, a wiki is one of the most diverse sites on the web that you can use to compile the various Web 2.0 technologies that you already find useful and functional for achieving language production and learning in your class into one easy site for you and your learners. Wikis can also be used in all levels of education from kindergarten to graduate school, and even with your department or coworkers. Wikis help organize, display, and create more information to be available for anyone who uses it. There are a multitude of elements that can go into making an effective wiki, but as stated above, the major decision in designing an effective wiki is to decide on the learning goals for your intended audience, and how to meet that purpose.

If your goal is exposing them to real-world examples of the target language, or even exposure to a dialect that is not a target language to discuss the concept of world Englishes, you can use a wiki to centralize the video, create a handout and follow up activities, and give further instruction for the next class. You can use a single wiki in your classroom with all students engaging with it and the teacher acting as a facilitator. Alternatively, you could create student group wikis and have four or five wikis in one class, or students themselves could take on the task of creating and maintaining a wiki. Additionally, you could use a wiki as a means of working towards centralizing and standardizing your department management or sharing system for teaching resources with fellow coworkers, but no matter how you choose to use it, for it to be successful everyone involved would need to be aware of what the goals and purpose of having the wiki are.

Examples
I have used wikis to organize the group projects that I needed to accomplish while getting my MA TESOL degree. I had a testing and analysis assessment class project where our group of four students had to create a test based on a specific grammar point in consultation with an appropriate teacher at the university. The test needed to have justification, be created, be analyzed, and be reported on. By creating a wiki, we had a group space that was visible to the general public, but we didn't tell anyone else that we created it, and I'm not aware of anyone who saw it during the time in use. We were able to write, add, organize, and edit everything that was needed to be able to create the test collaboratively and efficiently. In another class, we had to create a curriculum, and it was also very easy for this other group to all work together and to compile an entire curriculum with justification and details for why it was created the way that it was. Our groups were created by our professors under certain

guidelines, and it was fortunate that the groups that I was in accepted my idea of using a wiki, although the teacher never instructed us to use one. I learned about them and had to create one in a previous class before taking these classes, so I already had an opportunity to learn how to work with and use one. It is important that you take time before implementing them in a class to create a trial one to learn what you need to be able to do. Trial and error is always key when trying to adapt the curriculum, and any class can benefit from a wiki as long as there are clearly defined goals and a purpose in mind. For example, when teaching writing with a wiki I focus on getting students to produce written work of up to 200 words, but of course, depending on the needs of the class and the learning outcomes of the course each teacher will have their unique goals and results to focus on.

Effective Elements behind a Wiki:
Instructor Attitudes

Wikis give you the ability to create a unique online environment tailored to the needs that you have for your classroom. However, West and West (2009) state that "without any proper planning and familiarity with technology, wiki activities wouldn't be successful" (p.127). In addition, regardless of how digitally native your students may be, and used to using different technologies, this does not mean that they will just naturally be able to use a wiki without any extra instruction or guidance. Altanopoulou and Tselios (2017) stress that "perceived ease of use had a significantly positive effect on students' wiki attitude only in the pre-wiki scenario" (p. 142), which means that students will not always find a wiki easy to use. Their findings stress that if students do in fact have an overall positive view of its purpose (the tasks you use with intended goals with the wiki), then they will intend on use it. Any teacher can find a way to make a wiki useful for their students with enough creativity and focus on learning goals. Herraiz-Martinez (2018) also points out that "children are always willing to use computers, tablets, or phones in order to play" (p. 48), so using technology like this at any schooling level may encourage engagement, and "working with TBLT and technology is essential when learning the English language in EFL contexts" (p. 53).

Student Attitudes

Knowing a bit about student attitudes that has already been researched can help teachers to also better know how to design effective tasks that fit their wiki and class design or wiki purpose. Altanopoulou and Tselios (2018) came to the conclusions that students who exhibit extroverted personality traits had a negative correlation with perceived ease of use, and also that extroverted students had a negative correlation with academic performance (Altanopoulou & Tselios, 2015). This means that teachers need to strive to make things easy and not burdensome for all students when doing tasks associated with wikis. Group work is useful for creating learning and diversity of thought, so a teacher should help to create equal opportunities for all students to do well. Altanopoulou and Tselios (2018) suggest that "an effective group should not comprise too many students with a high degree of extraversion ... Moreover, students with [a] degree of agreeableness and emotional stability should be evenly distributed across the groups" (p. 144). This is because personality differences in your groups may allow for more positivity regarding your use of a wiki to be perceived in your classroom. It is important to note too that while this study contained 85 participants, it was predominantly women, so further research into students' perceptions of wikis among male students could be required.

It is difficult for every teacher to be aware of students' personalities and their intricacies but wikis do allow for a lot of customization and individualization of student tasks. Every teacher should provide activities at the beginning of a semester or term to try and find out information about their students so as to have some insight that they can later use to help them situate learners into productive groups for various classroom tasks. To do this, I give a short explanation of each of the eight multiple intelligences given in Gardner (2004), and have students rank 1 to 8 their order preference for learning according to the theory. I do this in order to determine how they think they like to learn.

Getting Started with Wikis
Wiki History
As previously mentioned, the most famous wiki is Wikipedia, and you can most certainly create the classroom goals that you want to meet by having students editing, adding, and/or monitoring content on Wikipedia. Wikipedia and the many wikis that compose the total of what Wikipedia represents are based off of the MediaWiki engine. Richardson (2009) details how school districts and various types of teachers have utilized Wikipedia to achieve educational goals. Sadly, many of the early wiki creation sites either no longer exist or no longer relate to creating wikis. But not to worry, there are still some good wiki creation sites with various options, and one can easily find one that fits their needs and goals as a teacher. PBWorks (formerly pbwiki.com) is a very good wiki creation site that is easy for both teachers and students alike to use.

PBWorks
Within the pbworks.com site, you can find a tremendous amount of information related to wikis used for industry and professional purposes as well as wikis for educational use. As of now (2019), PBWorks wikis can still be used for free as long as you only intend to use them for non-commercial purposes (more detail below). Free wiki sites for non-commercial or educational purposes are still limited, however, and the limitations and potentials of each type (both free and paid) are discussed below.

Getting Started

In order to create a free wiki for educational purposes from PBWorks, you must visit their website, then click 'Get Started' in the upper right corner, click the 'Edu Hub' icon, and you will be shown a breakdown of the 3 types of wikis that you can sign up for, with only one of them being free. It is advisable to get familiar with a free wiki before approaching a school board or department head asking for funds to use a more enhanced wiki. After getting proficient at using a free wiki and having demonstrated that it benefits teachers and learners, you are in a better position to argue for getting funds to expand and use wikis with more options.

Basic (Free)

The first step in how to make a wiki is to think of an easy-to-remember name for the class that you want to use it with. A free or Basic wiki gives you a workspace (wiki) to use and up to 100 users can join it. As well, you will receive 2 GB of storage space which you are free to use however you wish, and you can upload any file (Microsoft PowerPoints, audio files, handouts, and so on) but each file is limited to 50 MB. This means that most movie-length videos cannot be uploaded, so it will be demonstrated how best to use different internet tools so that your wiki maintains as much available storage as possible and allows you to use the bulk of it for essential files like handouts or class materials. You also have 'Limited customization,' 'Basic email support,' and 'No data export.' It is my opinion that a free wiki can nearly fit the needs of all teachers looking to improve their classroom through the use of the technology.

Classroom & Campus (Paid)

The other PBWorks wiki accounts are called Classroom and Campus, and are accessible for a fee. One big difference between the paid versions and the Basic/free version is that you are given 40 GB of storage space with each instead of only 2 GB. As well,

Practical and Innovative Applications for Wikis | 57

the Classroom and Campus versions allow for full customization (useful if you want to tailor things more within your wiki), provide 'Priority email support,' and 'Zip data export.' Classroom provides one wiki limited to 100 users (same as Basic), and Campus provides unlimited wikis with 1000 users under one account. You will have to decide if the increased storage, customization, support, data export, and more wikis and users make it worth the money for you and/or your organization.

Comparisons
Using a free wiki gives you plenty of potential to create a new and unique learning environment for your students, although it is possible to just take what you have, transfer or copy it to a new wiki and let your former students take over the wiki that they helped create. Or, you can have the students leave the wiki that you created and have new students join it in the next semester or term. Either way, you are limited to 2 GB or 40 GB of storage depending on if it is free or not. The only way to use any PBWorks wiki with more than 100 users is to get the Campus version.

If you work on a university campus or at any other educational institution and want to use the same wiki repeatedly semester after semester or term after term and still allow every student to stay on the wiki after they leave your class, this option may be something to consider, but as any full-time teacher knows, it doesn't take long to teach 1000 students, so even with Campus, a university or large institution teacher would find that they have reached the limit on users for this type of wiki possibly after just four or five years or even less. Some schools such as Hanyang University in Seoul and Ansan have developed a university wiki of their own, which is accessible from their home page (http://hanyang.ac.kr).

If your university's computer and software department is big enough, you might want to talk with them and explore the wikis that may be already available to you through your institution.

Learning management systems (LMS) are also widely implemented at universities and other educational institutions, so you might want to check with your school and see what wikis they might be able to make available to you.

Email, Accounts, and Permission Levels
Email
Using a PBWorks Basic account enables you to simply create student accounts, however, I feel this is only appropriate if you are teaching at a primary or secondary level institution. Even at the secondary level of language instruction at the middle or high school level, I would recommend giving a lesson on creating good and well recognized email accounts that students can use if they don't already have one. Of course, this should be done with considerations in line with your institution and its guidelines. It should also be noted that if students are in the European Union they are not legally permitted to use PBWorks or other similar sites unless they are 16 years or older.

If you are teaching at a tertiary institution it is highly recommended that even if students already have emails, that teachers should still go over what is considered a good and well created email that suits each student. It is my understanding that many students in Korea (at least) create what seems to be random strings of letters and numbers that can be sent to any internet user's spam folder when receiving an email. Email is still a frequently used web tool that is necessary to reap the benefits of all Web 2.0 tools that are available. If you are working with students who do not have emails or it is too complicated due to age or your institution, PBWorks still makes it easy to utilize a wiki by providing students with accounts through the wiki itself.

If students have emails and you make the wiki publicly visible, students can just look in the upper right corner of the wiki and see 'To join this workspace, request access'. After students join your wiki, they can just log in, which is also in the very upper right corner of the wiki. Students can then leave comments for the wiki administrator or you the creator. It is also possible to 'Contact workspace owner' which allows anyone who is not part of PBWorks to contact you.

Accounts

When using a PBWorks Basic account wiki intended for educational use, you can click on the 'Users' tab in the upper left corner set of tabs for your wiki, and then click 'Add more users'. A window will appear for you to 'Add Users to (your wiki name)' and a link to 'Create accounts for your students'. This brings you to a page that asks you for the number of student accounts that you need and also what level of user you want your students to be. 'Administrator,' 'Editor,' 'Writer,' or 'Reader' are the titles PBWorks assigns for permission levels for interaction with the wiki created. However, you can only create accounts through the wiki by assigning everyone as the same role in the first step, and Administrator is not allowed when creating accounts. These roles will be discussed below.

Permission Levels

Giving students the most responsibility, as in Editor or even Administrator may not be an issue, because in the classes I have taught using wikis I have found that students while interacting with a wiki will typically only do what is instructed and nothing more until you give them a purpose and motivation. Although, it is a fear that giving students administrative permission could allow them to remove students from the wiki so every teacher needs to think about how students will interact with the wiki, and I have not had any students cause 'chaos' or 'issues' when using wikis that I have created. This is the first step for setting up accounts and it is my strong opinion that even giving children specific permission levels that limit a wiki's usage will only prove to be demotivating, and less interaction with the wiki will result.

However, administrators can control every user's settings. That said, research is still needed for wikis in education and wikis in general concerning the nature of interactions and limiting a user's permission levels.

Clicking the 'Continue' button takes you to step 2 which is where you can input the names of your students and change default permission levels. The default is 'Writer,' however, 'Editor' will allow them to create pages and potential links to self-created pages depending on what you teach while using a wiki. At this point, it is possible to change individual users' permission levels one by one. They are also given a user name and password which will need to be given to them in some way. You can input your real student names and alter their username to teach them the basics of what can constitute a good email or future username when dealing with things online. Lastly, you are asked to double check the spelling for each student's information and click 'Create accounts', and once you have completed this information, you are given an option to print this list so you can make copies and distribute it to students, parents, and/or administration.

I believe that assigning every student as 'Editor' or even 'Administrator' with as much control as possible will not create chaos with your wiki; rather, it will possibly enable students to perform autonomous learning that could further aid in the educational benefits that you may be trying to achieve. Assigning student roles as 'Reader' only allows students to read pages and comment at the bottom of each page. Yet, will students do autonomous creation on their own without being instructed to do so? Perhaps, perhaps not, it's up to you to encourage it.

Using and Teaching with a Wiki:
Editing Pages
After you have created a wiki and your students join your wiki, it is important to go over how to use it, and the key aspect to note is page creation and how to edit pages. A good first week activity

is to have every student post a short personal introduction, and make sure that each student understands that they should write their introduction below the previous student's introduction. When this assignment is given, it is important to explain that only one student at a time can edit a single wiki page, so if they see a message such as 'This page is currently being edited,' they need to wait until the page is free for them to edit because that means a student is currently adding their information.

The Sidebar
A key feature every teacher needs to use with a PBWorks wiki is the 'Sidebar' on the right side of every page, and it is located in the same space on every wiki page when it is not being edited. Because it is located on every page, this makes it a key place for navigating the different pages of your wiki. You could put student links on your Frontpage, the first page that everyone sees when visiting the wiki, or if you are going to base your wiki off of every student having their own 'Homepage', people can navigate by following student created links, then you could put a link to every students' page in the sidebar and use the front page for class explanations that can be kept, changed, or added to.

Using and Learning
When you start using your wiki, having a first class with an overhead projector showing the students your wiki and how it works is highly recommended, along with a user manual for your particular wiki. As much as we might strive to have a completely paperless classroom, it is important to remember that some students may prefer having some kind of paper reference. If you are simply using a wiki for your own archiving, or possibly as a site for department-wide resources, first ask if your department wishes to make this public to all students or if you want it to remain private. It is completely possible for you to design a wiki that students do not even need to join and can just visit outside of

class to watch, listen, read, or download various activities that you want to make available to your students online. They could easily follow a calendar of videos that you post for your wiki and complete activities in class using a more traditional pen-and-paper approach.

Teacher as Facilitator

If you are going to use a wiki that all students join, or even a class where students create wikis themselves, it is best for the teacher to play the role of a facilitator. Herraiz-Martinez (2018) states that "the teacher is a facilitator who has all the information and who can give access to the different activities and tasks that are to be conducted through the computers" (p. 45), and while students can have complete access at all times to the wiki that you use, it is important that you assist them by taking on the role of a facilitator. It is necessary for any teacher to model a task so that students have a clear understanding of what needs to be done before they take on the task that you wish them to perform. Just because you model something on the class computer, or on student computers, this does not mean that you should not also distribute a handout to guide students in their learning. If it is possible, I would recommend using both English and your students' L1 so that they can fully understand the wiki terminology that they will need, since the vocabulary of wikis is technical and not widely used.

Storage & Embedding

Another factor to consider when having students using a wiki is the amount of storage involved with each task. Short audio files are usually not more than 1 or 2 MB, so it would be possible for a maximum of 100 students on a Basic wiki to all upload one audio file, or as many as a few especially if there are only 25 students or less using a single wiki. Any text documents can be created by simply writing to a wiki page instead of using Microsoft Word or other similar word-processing programs that would just make students go through the extra step of then cutting and pasting it or uploading it to the wiki. As a teacher, you should also consider what files you want to upload to a wiki, keeping in mind the free storage allocation if you or your school cannot allocate funds for the purchase of additional storage.

Not to fret though, it is possible to use many Web 2.0 tools to allow for student audio and video files to be displayed on your wiki with a few simple steps that will be discussed in the following section. If you have students making videos for things even as simple as just a Microsoft PowerPoint slideshow with no speaking, you can have students upload these to sites like YouTube or Vimeo, and then embed them into the wiki. It is my opinion that Vimeo helps to make students more comfortable with putting things online and I will explain why below. It is possible to embed any video on a wiki which will not use up storage space. SoundCloud and BandCamp are also sites that teachers and students can upload audio files to, and then embed these into a wiki as well to keep wiki storage space available. However, any site that allows you to embed things into your wiki requires someone to create an account and user ID as well as extra steps to display it on your wiki, and creating extra steps that students may view as mundane could lead them to finding wiki use disadvantageous and disagreeable for their learning. Careful attention to what your teaching goals are and the best most efficient way to complete these tasks are what could create a positive online learning environment for you and your students.

Evaluating:
Participation
Every teacher must consider what outcomes they are trying to achieve and how best to assign a value such as a grade to any activity done on a wiki. Wikis give you valuable insights into how students are using them through 'Page history' (a link on every

page), 'Page view count', 'Last date visited', and their email addresses and the approximate locations of their user profile information. This data allows you to determine if students are visiting the wiki, as well as what edits they have made to any page, which in turn can be utilized as part of a participation grade, depending on your syllabus and how you have planned to utilize the wiki. You could try any basic task such as the previously-mentioned self introduction on the FrontPage (also, the page that the 'Wiki' link in the upper left corner always takes you to) from each student as a beginning effort assessment. You can then utilize the 'Page history' link in the upper right corner of the section where words on the page are visible to access the date, time, and information concerning each user's edits of any page, and the completion of this assignment. I recommend, after having done so with my own students, that any teacher award points for effort when using a wiki, particularly at the onset, so that students can feel comfortable and not be pressured to perform.

Rubrics

If you want to use the wiki completely as a way to award online participation, you can come up with a few tasks that are easy to handle and then determine whatever percent of their grade you wish for this. When it comes to giving different grades on the assignments that students do on your wiki, many teachers and textbooks that teach about assessment (Brown, 2005; Finch & Shin, 2005; Hughes, 2003; Kent, 2017) advocate using a rubric. Several rubrics are available on a variety of topics by just doing a Google search, but I would definitely cover basic topics related to writing for the web in your class, particularly if you are going to assign webpage-based writing assignments. For example, students in Korea should be made aware of pushing 'Enter' only when they change topics so the spacing visible online viewed as a webpage looks like the standard writing format for them. Rubrics can be used for assessing the activities themselves such as a video or audio assignment, but you may learn that student use of the wiki and how things look vary from student to student so you may want to add parts to your lessons demonstrating how to use the wiki and internet effectively and include these parts into your rubric. Any rubric should of course be shown to your students, or they should at least be instructed on the guidelines that will be used with your wiki so they are aware of how you will assess them.

Checklists
Another easy way to assess wiki assignments instead of participation points or a rubric could be a checklist style of assessment, useful for assessing any task that might have a set of steps that students must complete to achieve a certain result. I have found this to be especially useful in my own teaching when concerned with students achieving the same results but not the same level of accuracy when performing a task. Deciding on your outcome goals and any set grade distributions that you need to follow (such as a curve for grade distribution) should be guided by whether you should just assign participation, follow a rubric, or use a checklist. The level of students and the differences in students in a class should also be used as a guide for how you approach this. It is highly recommended that teachers grade based on participation, at least in the beginning of using a wiki with students, even when the wikis may be made by the students themselves.

Using Various Web 2.0 Tools with a Wiki
A Changing Internet
As mentioned earlier, a Basic or free wiki has limited storage space and 2 GB of storage is not much given today's world of videos, audio files, and so much more. I'm sure that some teachers easily have over 2 GB of materials that they are currently using. Many of our students, depending on their age, probably have

over this amount of music. I would recommend that teachers use the storage for material that is specific to their wiki site and specific to content that is not possible to upload to other sites/platforms. The ones that have embedding features will be discussed below, but first the toolbar must be mentioned since this is the key to using many of these features with your wiki.

Toolbar
Almost everything available to you in Microsoft Word such as underlining, bolding, italicizing, various font styles, sizes, and colors, tables, lines, bullet points, making pages left/right/center justified, spell check, and other formatting options are all easily available when you click 'Edit' on a wiki. For any style of writing that you want to educate your students on, writing to a wiki page will give you options that fit your needs, and students can easily add pictures using URLs (Universal Resource Locators) or files that they upload. A picture set to 'Public' in privacy options on Facebook even gives you a URL that you can embed for pictures.

Insert
PBWorks wikis also have several easy options for you and your students to utilize which can make their lives easier than possibly working with embedding code. When you click on the 'Edit' tab for your wiki page, you can then simply click on the 'Insert' dropdown menu and find the 'Video' option which will allow you to simply copy and paste a URL link to a video file without needing to embed code. This works as a plugin for sites like YouTube, Vimeo, Flickr (for videos and pictures), Viddler (a healthcare community-building video site), Qik (Skype's new app), Hulu (an American TV and movie streaming site), or Animoto (another video creation site). With certain sites like Vimeo and YouTube, you can share the video from a certain point in playback, inserting the video at the point you set to be played. Vimeo also allows students to password-protect a video if they

don't want other people to see it, and you could simply ask them to share the password with you or the entire class if they are anxious about having something open to the public on Vimeo itself.

More Plugins

Within the 'Insert' menu in the toolbar, you can also see a 'More Plugins' dropdown menu. This menu includes options for 'Teaching Tools' (inserting an equation for math, or a footnote), 'HTML & Gadgets' (inserting a 'Google Gadget' and RSS feed (HTML meaning hyper-text markup language; and, RSS meaning real simple syndication), which you may be aware of and want to add to your wiki), a 'Video & Photo' option that allows you to 'Upload a video' (but this is only available with a paid version because currently you cannot upload any single file larger than 50 MB on a free wiki, which is almost any video), a 'Page information' menu ('Include another page', 'Recent visitors', 'Google translation', or '# of visitors'), and last is an "Interactive media" menu ('Skype' and 'Voki Speaking Avatar'.) With all of these options, and with so many websites currently just a click away from you, I am sure that you already have ideas for something you can try with a wiki. The menu just above 'More plugins' is the '< > HTML/JavaScript' option which lets you copy and paste any HTML or JavaScript that you find into your page as a plugin. An excellent example of HTML that you might want to include is available through slideshare.net because this site gives you the ability to upload all of your Microsoft PowerPoints to one site and then put them into your wiki by using an embedding code. If you ever think that you have encountered an error when trying to embed something using these options, just click on the '< > Source' button in the toolbar and try to insert it directly into the page that way as a last resort (for more on HTML capabilities, see Appendix A).

Audio

You can embed a variety of audio streams into your wiki such as any song, podcast, or story on SoundCloud or BandCamp. You can also embed a variety of audio news streams from sites such as pri.org, (Public Radio International), npr.org, (National Public Radio), or any other radio streaming site you can find an embedding code for, or you can embed the live YouTube streaming station in South Korea known as TBS e-FM by using the method described above, and many other radio stations and podcasts that may also have YouTube channels. As long as it plays audio and it has an embedding code, typically found if you look under how to share it, you can use it in your wiki. You also have the option of uploading an audio file that anyone can download and play on their computer or phone, or you can actually embed an audio file that plays directly when you click on a page. (See Appendix A on how to perform this action).

Embedding

An embedding code is simply HTML code, that is typically found on a website by clicking on the 'Share' button or feature below the media you are listening to, watching, or reading, you will see a line that looks like this: <iframe> ... </iframe>. This is your embedding code for whatever video, audio file, PowerPoint, or any other interesting thing you can put into a website. You can see the HTML language involved in your wiki pages when you are editing a wiki page by clicking the '< > Source' icon in the toolbar. This will show you where to put the embedding code, for example when looking at the source of a wiki page you can embed the code where you see: <p> </p>. You can also simply put any HTML coding you find useful on the internet directly into your page by inserting it after <p> and clicking 'Save'. You can then view whatever you embedded directly on your wiki. The ' ' in the HTML line does nothing and you can just add whatever embedding code before it or delete it without affecting your wiki page.

Comments Section
Every page on a wiki has a comments section at the bottom. You can easily create pages with audio news stories from reputable sites and have students answer questions that you list below the audio or video media in the comments section of a page. You could post a song with a page that displays a gap-fill exercise for words that you removed from the lyrics and have the students put their answers in the comments section. You can also link any website such as a news article and have them read all or a part of it and then comment on it.

One thing to remember, when inserting a link to a different webpage or even a wiki page, is to make sure that you 'Edit' the link with the option to open the webpage in another tab in an internet browser. This is important because anytime that someone navigates away from the page that you want them to see, it makes them less likely to return to the page that you wanted them to focus on, and having the new page in a second tab ensures that their current tab stays on the wiki page that they were previously at. As mentioned, the 'Sidebar' is a useful way for people to navigate and know how to find key pages on the wiki. Also, a user-permission level set to 'Reader' allows the user to still comment on every page as well as to see every page.

What Do You Need a Wiki to Do?
Whatever subject you happen to teach, a wiki can be useful, and it is likely that a teacher who teaches what you teach has already made a wiki to aid their students' learning. With the wide assortment of Web 2.0 tools that you probably are already using, you can easily centralize these and various media on a wiki. Once you have learned how to centralize all the things that you need for your classroom that are possible with a wiki, then I

recommend inviting students to join a wiki that you can use with them. If you are really dedicated, you can either create a class project where every student creates their own wiki, or they can create them in groups. If you notice that you quickly catch on to how you can use your wiki, and your students do too, it is an excellent opportunity to try and create an entire class that is based on wikis. I have taught a practical English writing class that was focused on business writing communication, and an academic writing class teaching the basics of citations and essays, and I have concluded that wikis can lend themselves to writing classes and that students will use them given the right motivation to learn. If you are well versed in computers and different Web 2.0 tools, it is also completely possible to make a class where students use wikis to encompass all of the various sites that I mentioned and any other ideas into their own wikis. When you have the possibility of designing an entire class around wikis, you can see truly great and amazing things arise from the creation process while blending technology seamlessly into student learning.

Conclusion

This chapter has detailed the beginning of wikis with Wikipedia and has demonstrated the capabilities of a PBWorks Basic wiki. Surely, wikis are here to stay and are beautiful things that if utilized effectively can change the world in leaps and bounds. Since all major Web 2.0 tools can be linked to, and a variety of media can be embedded or linked to from a PBWorks wiki, and as even more teachers learn about HTML (See Appendix A), the teaching potential with wikis is perhaps almost limitless.

References

Altanopoulou, P., & Tselios, N. (2015, November). How does personality affect wiki-mediated learning? In M. Auer, and S. Schreiter, *Proceedings of IMCL 2015 - 2015 International Conference on Interactive Mobile Communication Technologies and Learning* (pp. 16-18). Red Hook, NY. Curran Associates, Inc.

Altanopoulou, P., & Tselios, N. (2017). Assessing acceptance towards wiki technology in the context of higher education. *International Review of Research in Open and Distributed Learning, 18*(6), 127-148.

Anderson, C. (2006, May 8). Jimmy Wales. Time. Retrieved from http://content.time.com/time/specials/packages/article/0,2880 4,1975813_1975844_1976488,00.html

Anderson, M., Hitlin, P., & Atkinson, M. (2016, January 14). Wikipedia at 15: Millions of readers in scores of languages. Factank News in the Numbers. Retrieved from https://www.pewresearch.org/fact-tank/2016/01/14/wikipedia-at-15

Ayers, P., Matthews, C., Yates, B. (2008). *How Wikipedia Works And How You Can Be a Part of It*. USA: No Starch Press.

Barjami, L., & Ismaili, M. (2016). The role of video materials in EFL classrooms. International Conference on teaching and Learning English as an Additional Language, GlobELT. April 14-17. Antalya, Turkey. *Procedia – Social and Behavioral Sciences, 232*, pp. 502-506.

Brown, J. D. (2005). *Testing in language programs: A comprehensive guide to English language assessment*. New York, NY: McGraw-Hill.

Brookshire, B. (2018, February, 5). Wikipedia has become a science reference source even though scientists don't cite it. Scicurious, Science News. Retrieved from https://www.sciencenews.org/blog/scicurious/wikipedia-science-reference-citations

Cary, M. (2019a). esln312. Retrieved from http://esln312.pbworks.com

Cary, M. (2019b). Hanyang Multimedia Projects. Retrieved from http://hyumultimediaprojects.pbworks.com/w/page/45480965/FrontPage

Cary, M. (2019c). Practical English Writing. Retrieved from http://pracwriting.pbworks.com/w/page/18123420/FrontPage

Chew, E., & Ding, S. (2014). The zone of proximal and distal development in Chinese language studies with the use of wikis. *Australasian Journal of Education and Technology, 30*(2), pp. 184-200.

Dalby, A. (2009). *The World and Wikipedia: How We are Editing Reality*. USA: Siduri Books.

Engstrom, M., & Jewett, D. (2005). Collaborative learning the wiki way. *Tech Trends, 49*(6), 12-16.

Finch, A., & Shin, D. (2005). *Integrating teaching and assessment in the EFL classroom: A practical guide for teachers in Korea*. Seoul, Republic of Korea: Sahoipyungnon Publishing.

Garner, H. (2004). *Frames of mind: The theory of multiple intelligences* (20th Anniversary. Ed.). New York, NY. Basic Books.

Giles, J. (14 Dec. 2005). Internet encyclopedias go head to head. *Nature, 438*, 900-901. Retrieved from https://www.nature.com/articles/438900a

Herraiz-Martinez, A. (2018). Technology and task-based teaching (TBLT): Exploring pragmatics. *International Journal of Education and Development using Information and Communication Technology, 14*(2), 38-61.

Hughes, A. (2003). *Testing for Language Teachers* (2nd edition). Cambridge, UK: Cambridge University Press.

Kent, D. (2017). *Blogs and wikis (TESOL strategy guide, Book 6)*. Kindle Edition. Sydney, Australia: Pedagogy Press.

Kent, D. (2019). *Teaching in the time of digital language learning.* Plenary address – The fourth industrial revolution and education: Digital language learning and teaching. *TESOL-MALL graduate program, Woosong University symposium and KOTESOL DCC workshop.* Woosong University West Campus, June 01. Daejeon, The Republic of Korea. Retrieved from https://www.youtube.com/watch?v=wxKOdSaqpHs

Krashen, S. (1981). *Second language acquisition and second language learning.* Oxford, UK: Pergamon Press.

Leuf, B., & Cunningham, W. (2001). *The wiki way: Quick collaboration on the web*, (1st printing). USA: Addison Westley.

Leuf, B., & Cunningham, W. (2005). *The wiki way: Quick collaboration on the web*, (6th printing). USA: Addison Westley.

Malamed, C. (2019). *Using wikis for learning and collaboration.* The eLearning Coach. Retrieved from http://theelearningcoach.com/elearning2-0/using-wikis-for-elearning/

Matthew, K. I., & Callaway, R. A. (2009). Wiki as a collaborative learning tool in a language arts methods class. *Journal of Research on Technology in Education, 42*(1), 51-72.

Murugesan, S. (2007). Understanding Web 2.0. *IT Professional*, 9(4), 34-41.

Prensky, M. (2001). Digital natives, digital immigrants. *On the Horizon, 9*(5), 1-6.

Richardson, W. (2009). *Blogs, wikis, podcasts, and other powerful web tools for classrooms* (2nd ed.). Thousand Oaks, CA: Corwin Press.

Romeo, M. (2019, May 29). The farmer's story. On *Words from the brave.* Produced by Charmax, Published by Baco Records. Retrieved from https://www.youtube.com/watch?v=YhKdtIGG2AM

Skiena, S., & Ward, C. (2013). *Who's Bigger: Where Historical Figures Really Rank.* UK: Cambridge University Press.

TESOL International Association. Mission and values. TESOL International Association. Retrieved from http://www.tesol.org/about-tesol/association-governance/mission-and-values

Vygotsky, L. S. (1978). *Mind in society: The development of higher psychological processes.* Cambridge, MA: Harvard University Press.

Wales, J. (2004). Jimmy Wales. Wikiquote. Retrieved from http://en.wikipedia.org/wiki/Jimmy_Wales

West, J. A., & West, M. L. (2009). *Using wikis for online collaboration.* San Francisco, CA: Jossey-Bass.

Wikipedia contributors. (2019a, April 04). WikiWikiWeb. Wikipedia, the free encyclopedia. Retrieved from https://en.wikipedia.org/w/index.php?title=WikiWikiWeb&oldid=890985118

Wikipedia contributors. (2019b, June 24). List of wikis. Wikipedia, the free encyclopedia. Retrieved from https://en.wikipedia.org/w/index/php?title=List_of_wikis&oldid=903170950

Wikipedia contributors. (2019c, March 10). TESOL International Association. Wikipedia, the free encyclopedia. Retrieved from https://en.wikipedia.org/wiki/TESOL_International_Association

Wikipedia contributors. (2019d, March 3). Korea TESOL. Wikipedia, the free encyclopedia. Retrieved from https://en.wikipedia.org/wiki/Korea_TESOL

Willis, W. & Willis, J. (2012). *Doing tasked-based teaching. Oxford Handbooks for Language Teachers.* Oxford, UK: Oxford University Press.

Zokor, V. (2009). Factors affecting the way students collaborate in a wiki for English language. *Australasian Journal of Educational Technology, 25*(5), 664-665. https://doi.org/10.14742/ajet.1113

Appendix A
A Complex Creative Task using HTML with a Wiki

Audacity
In this section, I will describe in detail how to use audio recording software and HTML coding that is not well known to many educators, and how to create a complex multi-step task that can really enable students to use their creativity. In order to record audio and layer it, or add multiple tracks at different volume levels, you need to have software such as Audacity which is available for download from http://sourceforge.net/projects/audacity. It is a free open-source program available in many languages and it is not necessary for your students to know this program in English. It is important that you let your students know that you do not care about them using technologies in English, just that they are producing their own language in English.

Multi-tracks
With Audacity, students are able to add multiple tracks to audio recordings so they are able to talk over the top of a song, and both their voice and the song can be heard just like in a movie or podcast. It is possible for your students to download any song or video from YouTube using a wide range of downloader programs, sites, or even mobile apps. They certainly can use a song file that they already have as long as it fits your parameters for the assignment that you have given. I would prefer that they use an English-only song and not one that is primarily or entirely in their L1 (first language).

Once they have this file, they can add it to Audacity, then push 'Record' and it will add another track. Most laptops (notebook computers) have built-in microphones that work perfectly for this project. Students will need to adjust the volume of their songs and the level of their voices when recording so they may need to experiment with levels to find what is comfortable for their voice and the song that they or you have chosen.

Creativity and Confidence
For this type of project you could tell your students to pick their favorite English song and record a short introduction about themselves and why this is their favorite song. Teachers should tell their students that this introduction should serve as a general all-inclusive first encounter that anyone visiting their wiki page will hear as soon as they see the page. No one will see their face and will only hear the song that they picked and their voice layered over it. This can help to inspire creativity and confidence in students as long as they feel in control and capable of completing the task. Establish pathways to complete this task as easy as possible for them, both in walking them through the steps in class and giving them ways to understand it outside of class. Providing learners with a handout in English and in their L1 may increase the acceptance of doing this multi-step task.

Upload
Once the students have completed recording their voices over a song and have saved the audio file as an .mp3 file using Audacity, they will need to upload this file to their wiki. Music files are not large like video files, so it should be possible for many students to create and upload this file to a single class wiki that you have created. Once students have uploaded the file to the wiki, it gets a little tricky, but it basically involves inputting some specific HTML code related to the file and the wiki, and it will play once it is written correctly into the source. You will need to explain this clearly to your students but it is only one line of HTML code and will allow anyone who visits the page that the file is embedded in to hear it.

URL File

In order for students to embed the audio so that their file will play when someone visits their wiki page, they will need to copy and paste the code given at the end of this process into the source. You will need to click on the '<> Source' icon when you edit your page in order to paste the code into the source code. The URL you will have after you upload your mp3 file and the link to the file to be clicked on will look something like this:

> http://hyumultimediaprojects.pbworks.com/w/file/52524918/mp3%20file%20for%20audio%20project.mp3

Alter the URL

You will need to change the URL so /file/ is changed to /f/ and also delete the numbers after it, in this case, the 52524918. When you are editing the source code, you will need to change the URL to fit your file by changing the http:// to http%3A%2F%2F...mp3 and insert your changed file address so that in this case, it will look like this:

> http%3A%2F%2Fhyumultimediaprojects.pbworks.com/w/f/mp3%20file%20for%20audio%20project.mp3

Working Source Code

Once you have this source code changed according to the file that you added from your URL link, the completed source code can actually be embedded into *any* website and it will play as soon as someone clicks on the webpage. You will need to click '<> Source' when you edit your wiki page and insert it on a clean empty line while editing the source, or you can try using the '< > HTML/JavaScript' option in the 'Insert' dropdown menu, as previously mentioned.

78 | The Fourth Industrial Revolution and Education

The correct completed final source code looks like this:

```
<p><img class="pluginslug" src="/plugin_helper.php?plugin=external&amp;name=No+label&amp;html=%3Cembed+src%3D%22http%3A%2F%2Fhyumultimediaprojects.pbworks.com/w/f/mp3%20file%20for%20audio%20project.mp3%22+autostart%3D%22false%22+loop%3D%22false%22+width%3D%22300%22+height%3D%2242%22+controller%3D%22true%22+bgcolor%3D%22%23FFFFFF%22%3E%3C%2Fembed%3E&amp;warning=Note%3A+JavaScript+is+not+allowed+in+PBwiki+pages+and+will+be+stripped+out." alt="" /></p>
```

4. *Keep Talking and Nobody Explodes*: A Commercial Video Game with EFL Implications

Andrew Aguiar
TESOL-MALL Graduate Program, Woosong University
Nicole Shiosaki
Kongju National University

Introduction

The application of video games for teaching purposes has long been a point of interest for EFL (English as a foreign language) instructors. However, different games hold different potential for classroom integration. One commercial game that seems to be versatile is *Keep Talking and Nobody Explodes* (Steel Crate Games, 2015). This bomb-diffusing game provides students with the opportunity to produce language based on the principles of communicative language teaching and task-based language learning. The game was used with a small class of intermediate engineering students at a national university within the Republic of Korea, seeing students interact with each other in a meaningful way when they might otherwise have not. Paired with pedagogical theory, this game exhibits excellent potential for use with intermediate-and-above learners of English.

Keep Talking and Nobody Explodes: A Commercial Video Game with EFL Implications

Keep Talking and Nobody Explodes (Steel Crate Games, 2015) is a commercially produced video game made by Steel Crate Games and is available on numerous platforms including PC (Linux, MacOS X, and Windows), Nintendo Switch, PlayStation 4, Xbox, various virtual reality (VR) platforms, and a planned release onto Android and iOS. The game revolves around solving a series of procedurally generated modules (puzzles the must be completed to defuse a bomb) within a limited amount of time requiring two teams, one with a bomb and another with *The Bomb Defusal Manual* (Steel Crate Games, 2019), which contains the information required to defuse the bomb, to collaboratively work together to complete the task. The game requires each team to effectively communicate in order to succeed. As both teams only have part of the necessary information to complete the task, it makes the game an ideal information-gap task for EFL classrooms (Dormer, Cacali and Senna, 2017) and promoting verbal communication (Bodnar, 2017).

Digital Games and Education
Digital games have plenty of research in science, technology, engineering, and mathematics (STEM) education (Mayo, 2009; Annetta, Minogue, Homes and Chen, 2009) and language acquisition (Cornillie, Thorne and Desmet, 2012; Peterson, 2010; Reinders, 2012). Computer and video games' effects on language learning have also been thoroughly studied in an out-of-class social linguistic context (Thorne, Black & Skyes, 2009; Gee and Hayes, 2011; Gee, 2007) and the in-class context (Squire, 2005; Anderson, Reynolds, Yeh, & Huang, 2008; Annetta, Minogue, Homes & Cheng, 2009; Peterson, 2013, Reinders, 2012).

In the EFL context, a digital game that is either designed for L2 learning or a commercial-off-the-shelf (COTS) game may facilitate digital game-based language learning (DGBLL) where the game acts as a tutor (Cornillie et al., 2012). A COTS game that may be beneficial to language learners as a well-designed game is goal-oriented (Prensky, 2001) and provides scaffolding to aid the player in learning the game and the language of the game (Gee, 2007; Squire, 2005). COTS are user-centered (Gros, 2007) and typically fall into the teaching category of task-based language teaching (TBLT; Cornillie et al., 2012; DeKanter, 2004), which makes use of tasks that require real-world language in order to be accomplished (Van den Brandon, 2006).

Dormer et al. (2017) state that *Keep Talking and Nobody Explodes* (Steel Crate Games, 2015), a COTS game, fits well into the TBLT approach for EFL as the game is designed to be an information-gap task. Furthermore, Bodnar (2017) states that the game promotes verbal communication in an authentic way. The game lends itself well to the practicing of language for intermediate English speakers in a university context (Dormer et al., 2017). However, if not framed well, the learners may not see the relevance of playing the game in their language learning context (Dormer et al., 2017), which may indicate that a better framework can be developed around the game.

Pedagogical Implications
Communication
Keep Talking and Nobody Explodes' (Steel Crate Games, 2015) gameplay revolves around communication. If the players are able to communicate well, they will succeed in solving the task within the allotted time. The modules (puzzle types) each require descriptions and imperative language as well as specific language for each module as discussed in the implementation section.

Feedback
Feedback occurs as either in-game tactile feedback, through the strike system (when the players make a mistake in a module, the game makes a buzzing sound and an 'x' appears above the bomb timer), or through uptake feedback between players. For example, if the defuser does not thoroughly describe the word in the display for the 'Who's on First' module, the experts will need to ask for more information.

Non-commercial Licensing for Educational Use
Steel Crate Games (2018) state that *Keep Talking and Nobody Explodes* (Steel Crate Games, 2015) may be used for educational purposes (making and implementation of lesson plans) under a

non-commercial-use license. However, they also state that a copy of the game is to be purchased for each instance that the game being played at the same time. For example, if a class of twenty students formed groups of five, four copies of the game should be purchased.

Seven Basic Modules

Though there are fourteen modules included in the game, not all of them are well suited for language learning. For example, some modules are designed purely to waste time. However, there are seven modules (The Button, Keypad, Wires, Simon Says, Maze, Memory, and Who's on First) that appear in the early levels of the game that work well in the language-learning context. Before playing the game, these modules can be prepared for by analysing the language required to solve each information-gap task generated by the game. The following sections provide a brief explanation of the rules for these seven basic modules.

Wires

The first module outlined in *The Bomb Defusal Manual* (Steel Crate Games, 2019) is Wires, which requires the defuser to cut the correct wire in order to solve the module. There are three to six wires of various colors (including red, white, blue, black and yellow) that may be generated on this module. The defuser must provide information pertaining to the number of wires and their colors to the expert team, who then need to read through a series of conditions to determine which wire must be cut in order to solve the module. In addition, certain conditions require more information from the defuser in order to solve the module. For instance, if there are five wires and the last wire is black, the experts need information pertaining to the bomb's serial number which is hidden somewhere on the bomb.

The Button

The Button module is a two-step puzzle where the button needs to be identified first and then the color. For the first step, the best description of the button needs to be found, and then the instructions need to be followed.

Keypad

The bomb will have four symbols, and only one column in the manual will have all four symbols. The symbols on the bomb should be pressed in the order from top to bottom that they appear in the column.

Simon Says

Simon Says is a simple pattern repetition puzzle. However, each color represents a different significance which can be determined by reading the manual.

Who's on First

Who's on First is another multi-step module. This module has a display screen along the top and six buttons arranged into two columns beneath it. The screen shows a word and the buttons are each labelled with different words. This module has two corresponding pages in the manual. On the first page, there are images for each possible word in the display and an eye shape in one of the buttons. The second page of the module has a table of words that appear on the buttons in the first column and a list of different words in the second column.

The defuser needs to read the word on the display to the experts. Then, the experts must use this word to identify which button the defuser needs to read back to them. After the defuser reads the word to the experts, they will read words from the corresponding list. The defuser needs to press the first button that contains a word from the list.

Memory

The Memory module is a five-stage task, with the stage that the players are on being shown on the right side. Whenever a mistake is made, the player goes back to stage 1. The defuser reads the number in the display and the experts tell him or her which button to press. Then they move to stage two, then three, and so on. The defuser will need to remember the button that he or she pressed at each phase.

Maze

The Maze module requires the defuser to navigate a maze without being able to see the walls by communicating with the experts who can see the walls, but don't know which maze or the location of the defuser in the maze. In order to determine which maze, the defuser needs to describe the location of the circles in the table of dots. These mazes can be rotated. Once they have identified the maze, they need to describe where the white light, the starting location, and the red arrow, the ending location, are on in the maze. Once they know these locations, the experts need to guide the defuser from the white light to the red arrow.

Pedagogical implementation

Keep Talking and Nobody Explodes (Steel Crate Games, 2015) was implemented by one of the researchers in an open subject elective class to five students in a Korean national university campus that specializes in teaching engineering. Classes were forty minutes every weekday throughout a normal semester. As the students were engineers, and the game involves technical discourse, it seemed like a good match. Furthermore, the students in this class were interested in talking, but too shy to talk to each other. Lastly, the students were interested in computer games and some were familiar with *Keep Talking and Nobody Explodes*, but had never played it before.

Pre-teaching

While Dormer et al. (2017) focused on a task and modelled it in their implementation of *Keep Talking and Nobody Explodes* (Steel Crate Games, 2015), pre-teaching to provide initial scaffolding could also a viable approach. Furthermore, in order to avoid the major difficulty increase, only the first seven modules (Wires, The Button, Keypad, Simon Says, Maze, Memory and Who's on First) were implemented in our context. This was achieved through selecting an early level in the game (level 2.3) as the end goal for the lessons. Furthermore, as not all modules were taught, not all of the pages of *The Bomb Defusal Manual* (Steel Crate Games, 2019) were relevant. The required pages necessary to complete up to level 2.3 (1-11, 15, 21-23) were printed to make a modified version of the manual for the lessons described below.

Introducing the Premise and Rules of the Game

In order to be able to play the game effectively, the students were introduced to the game and the game manual (Steel Crate Games, 2019). The game was introduced by showing the trailer for the game, which can be found on the game's official website (keeptalkinggame.com). The students were then asked to try to guess the premise of the game based on the contents of the trailer before starting the game.

Once the general concept of the game is understood by the students, they are to be given the modified version of *The Bomb Defusal Manual* (Steel Crate Games, 2019). If necessary, run the manual through a lexical indexing website and give the students a list, found in the manual, of difficult vocabulary for their level. The students can turn this list into a glossary to refer to during the game if needed.

The students must read the third and fourth page of the manual as this informs them of the rules of the game. In particular, this page talks about the loss conditions of the game (running out of time or making too many errors). The example bomb (see page 3 of Steel Crate Games, 2019) shows the students where modules, serial numbers, ports and batteries may generate. Furthermore, this page mentions that the modules present on the bomb may be solved in any order. The fourth page explains that the LED light in the corner of a module indicates that a module is complete or incomplete depending on the color (green for complete, red for incomplete). From reading and discussing pages three and four of the manual together as a class, the students should know what they need to do to win and what will cause them to lose.

Each module that the students will encounter while playing the game should be examined as a class. As students will need to not only learn the rules of the puzzles but do so in a second language, it is fair to help them understand the module rules prior to playing. Some possible explanations are as follows.

Wires

The Wires module uses conditional and conditional imperatives, and these can be explained by using a flowchart (Figure 1) in conjunction with the information on page 5 of the manual (Steel Crate Games, 2019). The employment of a flowchart aids the students by providing them with a visual representation of the information presented in the bomb manual. If necessary, the students could fill in a flow chart using the information from the manual, or information that mimics the style of the manual.

The Button

Useful phrases to ensure they understand are "press and hold", "release when" and '#' in any position. At an intermediate level, the language required to complete this module likely does not need additional practice beyond the phrases above. Furthermore, this module is best learned by trying the module itself rather than pre-teaching it.

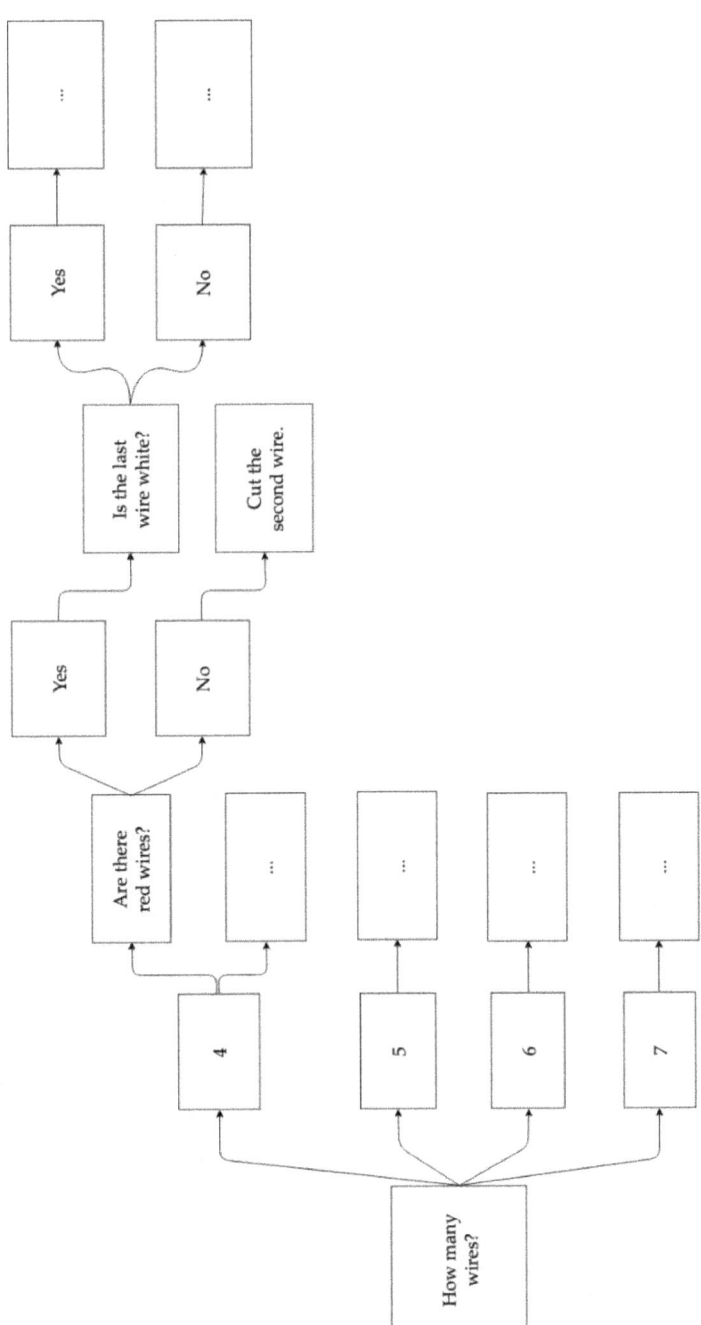

Figure 1. An example and incomplete flowchart useful for explaining the wire module

Keypad

While the keypad module is straightforward in terms of mechanics, the language required to relay information from the defuser to the experts may require practice. Students need to be equipped with descriptive-language terms and be able to make sure of similes in order to efficiently describe the symbols. This could be done over a forty-minute lesson as described in the additional activity lesson plan (Appendix A).

Simon Says

The Simon Says module is also straightforward in terms of mechanics and language, and students should be made of aware of the difference between vowels and consonants in order to determine which chart to follow in *The Bomb Defusal Manual* (Steel Crate Games, 2019).

Who's on First

There are several challenging aspects of this module. First, is the usage of homophones. Throughout the module there are several homophones that require both the defuser and experts to communicate clearly. For instance, the displayed word could be "you are," "your," "you're" or "ur." An additional issue that may be difficult for Korean EFL students is the inclusion of "lead" with "led," "read," "reads" with "reeds," and "leads" with "Leeds." Thus, it is important to not only make students aware of homophones, but also practice pronunciation of the l and r sounds. Expressions like, "How do you spell it?" and "Say it in a sentence" may help to give clearer descriptions. Since this module requires a lot of language in order to successfully complete it, a lesson about homophones and the l and r sounds should be taught (Appendix B). Making use of blogs, such as Homophone Weakly (Warden, 2015) and pronunciation charts (Hewings, 2004), may help build students' awareness of the existence of homophones as well as to their own pronunciation.

Memory

Ordinal and cardinal numbers make up the majority of the language needed for the Memory module, and as such, it is important to outline the differences in usage between the two numbering systems.

Maze

Language required to navigate the Maze module come in the form of describing locations on a grid and giving directions, and although coordinates may be used for the description of grid locations, description via rows and columns using ordinal numbers allows for more diverse applications throughout the game. For instance, rows and columns are also useful for describing the small table in Who's on First, and ordinal numbers can be used in every module described above. A lesson plan for teaching locations in grids and tables is included in Appendix C.

Giving directions is likely something that students are already familiar with. As such, this part of the module shouldn't be difficult if they are shown the similarity between phrases learned in class such as 'go two blocks north,' with in-game applications like 'go up two spaces.'

Playing the Game in Class

Once students are familiar with the language required to play the game and the rules of each module, they can play the game. Have the students play through level 1.1 to remind them of the rules of the game. Playing level 1.2 introduces the controls for the game, and if the class size allows it, each student should try this level. The controls vary based on the platform that the game is played on, so please see the in-game instructions for your particular system. Regardless of the system, the controls are simple and will have a button to select and do actions, a button to cancel, and a way to rotate the bomb.

Divide the class into the two roles, the defuser and the expert. The sizes of the group can vary based on the number of students in the class and the confidence of the students. For the defuser role, one or two students is probably optimal. Assign one student to be the head of the experts to relay the instructions to the defusers.

Next, the instructor should have the students play the game, and it will probably take a few rounds for the students to understand the puzzles. Start with level 1.3. Once they are confident with the controls and three initial puzzles, move on to level 2.1. If they are extremely confident try level 2.3.

After everyone has had a chance to play the game, the session can be concluded with discussion. The students should explain in their own words what they did, and discuss how they might use the game language for their daily lives. Possible answers may be that it helps them with their reading, giving descriptions, and giving and following directions. This debriefing stage is very important as it gives the students a chance to find relevance in the task that they have just completed, which is an issue of implementation in other EFL classes (Dormer et al., 2017).

Results

After the students learned about the rules for the individual modules and the language required to solve some of the more difficult modules, the students played the game. The language of the game was not an issue for the intermediate students, but for the low-intermediate and high-beginners, pre-teaching the language should have been done. The hardest part about the game was learning how certain modules worked. For instance, the button module had many errors, not due to language but due to students immediately releasing the button after pressing it rather than holding it down and providing more information.

Conclusion

Keep Talking and Nobody Explodes (Steel Crate Games, 2015) lends itself well to EFL classrooms (Dormer et al., 2017). Furthermore, usage in the classroom may be enhanced by providing scaffolding through teaching and practicing the language necessary to complete the modules before playing it. The game seems to be well-suited for review of common language patterns covered in the EFL classroom, as well as for a fun time-filler activity that promotes a lot of verbal communication within the classroom.

References

Anderson, T. A. F., Reynolds B. L., Yeh, X. P., & Huang, G. Z. (2008). Video games in the English as a foreign language classroom. *Second IEEE International Conference on Digital Game and Intelligent Toy Enhanced Learning, 199-192*, Banff, Canada

Annetta, L. A., Minogue, J., Homes, S. Y., & Cheng, M. T. (2009). Investigating the impact of video games on high school students' engagement and learning about genetics. *Computers & Education, 53*(1), 74-85.

Bodnar, J. (2017). *Talk it out: Promoting verbal communication through virtual reality games* (Unpublished masters thesis). Victoria University of Wellington, New Zealand. Retrieved from http://researcharchive.vuw.ac.nz/handle/10063/6890

Cornillie, F., Thorne, S. L., & Desmet, P. (2012). Digital games for language learning: From hype to insight? *ReCALL, 24*(3), 243-256.

DeKanter, N. (2004). Gaming redefines interactivity for learning. *TechTrends, 49*(3), 26-31.

Dormer, R., Cacali, E., & Senna, M., (2017). Having a blast with computer-mediated information gap task: *Keep Talking & Nobody Explodes* in the EFL classroom. *The Language Teacher, 41*(4), 30-32.

Gee, J. P. (2007). *What video games have to teach us about learning and literacy.* New York, NY: Palgrave Macmillan

Gee, J. P., & Hayes, E. R. (2011). *Language and learning in the digital age*. London, UK: Routledge.

Gros, B. (2007). Digital games in education: The design of game-based learning environments. *Journal of Research on Technology in Education, 40*(1), 23-38.

Hewings, M. (2004). *Pronunciation practice activities.* Cambridge: Cambridge University Press.

Mayo, M. J. (2009). Video games: A route to large-scale STEM education? *Science, 232,* 79-82.

Peterson, M. (2010). Massively multiplayer online role-playing games as arenas for second language learning. *Computer Assisted Language Learning, 23*(5), 429-439.

Peterson, M. (2013). *Computer games and language learning.* New York, NY: Palgrave Macmillan.

Prensky, M. (2001) *Digital game-based learning.* New York: McGraw-Hill.

Reinders, H. (2012). *Digital games in language learning and teaching.* London, Macmillan

Squire, K. (2005). Changing the Game: What Happens when Video Games Enter the Classroom? *Innovate: Journal of Online Education, 1*(6).

Steel Crate Games. (2015). *Keep talking and nobody explodes* [puzzle game]. Ottawa, Canada: Steel Crate Games.

Steel Crate Games. (2018). Non-Commercial FAQ. Keep talking and nobody explodes. Retrieved from https://keeptalkinggame.com/non-commercial-use

Steel Crate Games. (2019). Keep talking and nobody explodes: Bomb defusal manual (Vers. 1 Rev. 3). Retrieved from http://www.bombmanual.com

Thorne, S. L., Black, R. W., & Skyes, J. M. (2009). Second language use, socialization, and learning in internet interest communities and online gaming. *The Modern Language Journal, 93,* 802-821.

Van den Branden, K. (Ed.). (2006). *Task-based language education.* Cambridge: Cambridge University Press.

Warden, B. (2015, April 26). Dear & Deer. Homophones, Weekly. Retrieved from http://homophonesweakly.blogspot.com/2015/04/dear-deer.html

Warden, B. (2019). Homophones, Weekly. Retrieved from https://homophonesweakly.blogspot.com

Wikipedia contributors. (2019, June 20). Doge (meme). Wikipedia, the free encyclopedia. Retrieved from https://en.wikipedia.org/w/index.php?title=Doge_(meme)&oldid=902661342

Appendix A
Activity One: The Keypad

Target Language Skills
Describing unusual shapes using metaphors and descriptive adjectives.
- *Upside down, mirrored, backwards, right-side up, normal, sideways, rotated (counter- clockwise), twisty, curly, straight, stuck together.*
- *It looks like ____*
- *It looks like ____ but ____.*
- *It looks like ____ with ____.*
- *Is it (color)?*
- *Does it look like ____?*
- *Is there also ____?*

Introduction (5 minutes)
Draw a symbol on the board and ask the students to try to describe it. Let them attempt for a few moments, write down any words or phrases that they come up with that are effective.

Lesson Body Part 1 (15 minutes)
Draw the students' attention, and explain that you will introduce some phrases and vocabulary to help them describe types of shapes.

For example, draw the letter 'R' on the board in different rotations. Then, draw shapes to describe twisty, curly, straight and stuck together.

Next, introduce some phrases that might help students practice the use of these descriptions. Introduce the 'it looks like ____' phrases, and illustrate this with images such as a shiba inu meme

(Wikipedia contributors, 2019) or pareidolia images to demonstrate the meaning.

Then use symbols like theta to explain:
    It looks like _____ with _____.
    It looks like <u>a circle</u> with <u>a dot in the middle</u>.

Use an upside down R to explain:
    It looks like _____ but _____.
    It looks like <u>an R</u> but <u>it's upside down</u>.

Lesson Body Part 2 (5 minutes)
Put two or three symbols on the board and write one sentence beside them that could describe either.

Example:

    Ǔ   ǔ   Ũ   *it's like a U with a fist in the air.*

    How can we determine which one it is?

    Try asking clarifying questions such as
- *Is it black?*
- *Is it a big U?*
- *Does it have a little squiggly hat?*

96 | The Fourth Industrial Revolution and Education

Lesson Body Part 3 (10 minutes)
Put a list of symbols on the screen and have a set of cards with the same symbols on them (given in Figure A1). Have one student secretly draw a card. They need to try to describe the symbol that they drew and the other students need to guess which card it is.

Have the card-holding student describe the card using 3 sentences, then allow the other students to ask clarifying questions.

§	¢	⌧	Ø
ĉ	ë	Ė	ə
ɖ	ɤ	f	6
≡	⇝	ɸ	3
æ	ң	ӥ	J
‖	≡	☺	☻

Figure A1. A sample of symbols that students may use to practice descriptions

Appendix B
Who's on First?

Target Language Skills
Differentiating between homophones and other similar sounding words, and pronunciation (especially of words with *r* and *l* in them):
- *How do you spell it?*
- *Can you give me an example of it in a sentence?*

Introduction (5 minutes)
Visit the blog Homophones Weakly (Worden, 2019). Select a few images that you feel might be particularly interesting to learners and have the students read the titles on the images and try to explain the differences.

Lesson Body Part 1 (15 minutes)
With pictures or words, it isn't too hard to see the difference between them, but how about if you just say them? If I say *'bear'* do I mean *'bear'* or *'bare'*? How can you tell? A couple of options exist. In real life the main one is context, or the surrounding words and what their meanings are. For example, *'I can see a running bear.'* vs. *'I saw you running bare.'*

Next, have the students brainstorm as many homophones as they can, then come up with a sentence showing the difference between them (e.g., you're, your; there, their, they're; see, sea, c; red, read (past form); eye, aye, I.)

Lesson Body Part 2 (10 minutes)

It is hard to hear and make the difference between *l* and *r* but it is there. Tongue position and air flow is a useful way to try and introduce the way to make the sounds. Have the students try saying some [*r*] and [*l*] minimal pairs (e.g., rate/late, alive/arrive, light/right, glass/grass, brush/blush, free/flee, lice/rice, flee/free, law/raw).

However, because it is hard, and the game requires you to know exactly which words you are using, asking for the spelling or giving the spelling is acceptable.

Lesson Body Part 3 (5 minutes)

As two partners, one faces the board and the other faces away. On the board write several homophones and *l*/*r* words. The student facing the board must try to explain the word.

Appendix C
Who's on First? and Maze

Target Language Skills
Describing the location of things using a table and some other useful phrases:
- *Where is it?*
- *It's in the bottom left/top right/third from the left/second from the top drawer.*
- *First, second, third...*
- *Imperatives and directions (e.g., go left, press the third button.)*

Introduction (5 minutes)
Show the students a picture of a bookshelf with several things inside it (Figure A2) and ask them to tell you where the gray book is. Where is the white box? Where are the orange books? Accept however they try to express it, and explain that we will look at another way.

Figure A2. An example bookshelf image for describing locations of objects

Lesson Body Part 1 (15 minutes)

Provide the handout on how to describe tables to other class members as found in Appendix D.

Explain how to make sentences using the patterns below:
- It's in the down/across column.
- It's in the left/right column, and the top/middle/bottom row.
- It's [ordinal number] from the bottom/top and [ordinal #] from the left/right.
- It's in column [ordinal number] and row [ordinal number] It's in the down/across column.

Review ordinal numbers.

Return to the bookshelf image (Figure A2).

Have the student(s) describe where things are using this strategy.

Lesson Body Part 2 (15 minutes)

Tell the students that you want to go somewhere that they know the location of.

Tell them that you don't know where it is and that you need them to give you directions. Because they are intermediate, they should be aware of the vocabulary already.

Attempt to get them to use ordinal numbers as transitions.

Make sure that they know how to count blocks/spaces. First, (subject) + verb in infinitive form + object.

Conclusion (5 minutes)

Ask the students to answer the following two questions, and give them a minute to think about it then ask them to share their answers.
1. In your own words, explain what we did today.
2. In your opinion, how might you use this in conversations or daily life? (e.g., *explain where things are, describing data in tables, giving directions.*)

Appendix D
How to Describe Tables

Use the expression:
- *It's in the down/across column*
- *It's in the left/right column, and the top/middle/bottom row.*

1↓ 2→	Left	Right
Top		
Middle		
Bottom		

Figure A3.1. Examples of how to describe the contents of columns and rows found in a table to other class members

Use the expressions:
- *It's [ordinal number] from the bottom/top and [ordinal #] from the left/right.*
- *It's in column [ordinal number] and row [ordinal number].*

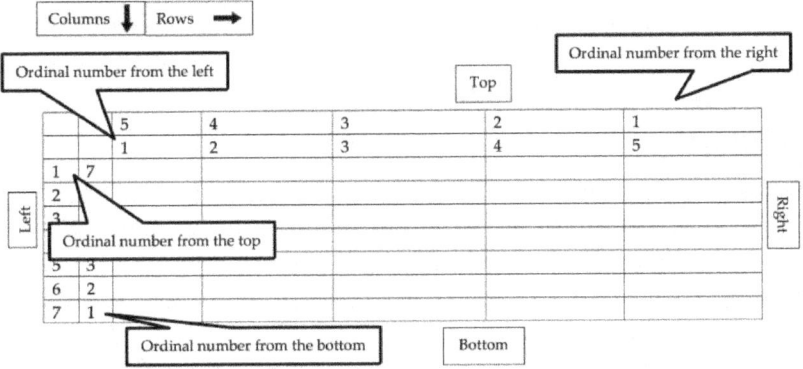

Figure A3.2. Examples of how to describe the placement of content found in the columns and rows of a table to other class members

5. *Explain Everything* in the English Classroom

Dilbar Shermatova
TESOL-MALL Graduate Program, Woosong University

Recent years have seen a growing need for the integration of technology and pedagogy that assists with developing student cooperation in the language teaching classroom (Glover, Miller, Averis, & Door, 2005). The use of interactive whiteboards and applications is claimed to be a primary assistant for teachers (Bell, 2002), and one that may help in this regard. *Explain Everything* (2011) is just such an interactive whiteboard platform where both teachers and students, or students by themselves, can work collaboratively in real-time. The application provides a means of breathing new life into teacher presentations, so that they become engaging for learners, while also focusing on aspects of audio- and visual-based collaboration. The significance then, for teachers of English to speakers of other languages (TESOL), is that this tool can be used to help engage students of any age level in the learning experience in both novel and interesting ways as students have a chance to create interactive activities to boost their foreign language learning. This chapter aims to explore the potential of the *Explain Everything* (2018) application, and how it can be applied in the English language learning classroom when using multiple mobile devices with students.

Introduction

The use of effective technology is considered to be one of the key factors that influence learner motivation, along with parental support, and teacher encouragement and skills (Beeland, 2002). Wishart & Blease (1999) also claim that a classroom environment where technology is applied innovatively is responsible for improving learning and teaching.

One of the many forms of technology now available for use by teachers with their learners in the classroom is interactive whiteboards. Those whiteboards are likely able to help deliver significant education potential to cover the needs of students with diverse learning styles and they may help serve to engage students during their foreign language learning process (Beeland, 2002). An interactive whiteboard is a means of technology that began to be used in classrooms in the late 1990s. It can be either a combination of a computer, an actual whiteboard, and a projector, or a standalone touchscreen computer that is capable of operating independently of any other device or system.

Although an interactive whiteboard brings a lot of opportunities for teachers to intersect technical and pedagogical interactivity with each other, there are questions: Are those whiteboards certainly used interactively? Can a big single screen for a number of students and a teacher be interactive? If we consider practicality, it is far more unlikely to be effective. This is where a multi-device approach for interactive whiteboards can probably provide solutions to these questions.

One interactive whiteboard platform available on the screen of mobile devices is *Explain Everything* (2011). It has all the features of a traditional interactive whiteboard but it can be used across a variety of different tablets, phones, or computers. The application arose from an initiative created by Gonczarek, Sliwinski, and Richards (Explain Everything, 2018). It is available for a number of platforms including Android, iOS, and the Windows operating system. It can be accessed freely, or one's account can be updated with extra features via paid services for individuals and groups.

This interactive whiteboard possesses huge potential for providing support to students and educators in terms of being able to create interactive activities and videos, and animations to explain concepts to others. *Explain Everything* (2011) allows users to import a variety of file formats for audio, images, and video, to Microsoft PowerPoint, and other file formats from local devices or from other locations such as email, Dropbox, and Google Drive. It also allows for the exporting of images or Adobe PDFs, as well as projects and videos to places such as YouTube, Facebook, and Messenger, and so on. The .XPL project files that are created by the application can also be shared with others for collaboration. The internet can be browsed from within the application, and specific parts can be explained using the drawing and highlighting tools available. What makes recording in *Explain Everything* (2011) remarkably useful for knowledge sharing is that it can capture the whole process on the screen in real time while one is recording audio with the click of a button below the whiteboard screen. Besides these features, the *Explain Drive* cloud storage solution is able to save all projects created while using *Explain Everything* (2011).

How does *Explain Everything* suit students with different learning styles?

According to Peacock (2001), learning styles in EFL classrooms are students' "natural, habitual and preferred ways" of acquiring and processing foreign languages. Reid (1995) classified learning styles into six types:

1. Visual (they prefer to learn with pictures, images, colors, maps and so on);
2. Auditory (they mostly learn by listening and speaking);
3. Kinesthetic (learning occurs through experiences, participation, discovery);
4. Tactile (they remember things better when they are involved in hands-on work, physical movement by touching and doing things themselves);
5. Group (they learn better in a group collaboration); and
6. Individual (they prefer studying alone).

Reid also states that students learn and engage much better when the content being taught matches with their learning styles. It is also technology that provides opportunities for teachers to meet the needs of students with various learning styles through the use of, and exposure to, multiple media (Bryant & Hunton, 2000).

In terms of this, *Explain Everything* (2011) can be used to deliver tutorials and instructions in a variety of ways stemming from the learning styles of those in the class. For example, accessing different images, including clip art, and videos, and presenting information graphically using a variety of colors and animation to display content, with audio recording, and importing different sounds or music to the project useful to support multimodal learning, visual and auditory learners. Due to its touch recognition, tactile learners can benefit from touching and marking content at the board using their fingers to navigate. Students can also be engaged in both team work or individual assignments when completing activities while using this application.

Explain Everything for online collaborative learning

Online collaborative learning is defined as a learning process where learners work in groups virtually to study a topic, solve complicated questions and accomplish authentic tasks (Herrington, Oliver, & Reeves, 2003; Herrington, Reeves, Oliver, & Woo, 2004). In such processes the teacher is likely to act as a facilitator rather than being an active deliverer of knowledge, and that much emphasis needs to be placed on engaging in language use along with real-life activities such as problem-solving and communication-based tasks instead of rote learning, and memorization-based activities. So too, collaborative group projects provide benefits to learners beyond what they would acquire working on their own (Henke, Locander, Mentzer, & Nastas, 1988). In their research, Mercier, Vourloumi, & Higgins (2017) found that students react more often to the ideas put forward by other learners than they do to those offered by instructors. This shows that students consider other learners input when working together, and this can help solidify comprehension. But no matter how highly group collaboration is valued by students, their lack of interest in engaging with team members has always been a problem for teachers. If we consider the fact that students of today's classrooms are 'digital natives', integrating technology into group projects can be an effective factor to drive learners' attention towards collaborative teams (Beldarrain, 2006).

Kathleen, with four years of teaching experience in the United Kingdom, participated in a study of primary school teachers' understanding of the interactive whiteboard as a tool for children's collaborative and knowledge-building (Warwick & Kershner, 2008). She found that interactive whiteboards are efficient for engaging students in collaborative work, reducing the time that it takes for all pupils involved to gain access to the information that they need to start a task, and allows much more of the class time to be spent on collaborative discussion.

As teamwork requires equal contribution of members, it is important for instructors to find a tool that is not only interactive, but enables several users to make changes simultaneously in whiteboard sessions. In this regard, while students are making use of the collaboration tools found in the *Explain Everything* (2011) application, they can work all together on the same canvas of the same project, and all the changes and contributions made in the project by different users can be visible to each other in real time. In order to create a group project, a teacher or any student first opens a new project canvas on the platform as a host. Before inviting session participants, the host should determine participants' privileges: whether they can just view, edit the board, download the project on their devices after the collaboration ends, or use voice communication while they are working together. The interactive whiteboard allows the host to invite participants for free. Members can join the project in three ways:

1. Participants enter the code sent by the group administer to the 'Enter CODE' field in the top right corner of the screen in the home page of the board;

2. Members can be invited via their email by the group host who started the project, and a confirmation email, including a code, is then sent to them, and allows them to start taking part in the team work by tapping 'Join with the invitation code'; and
3. A group administrator sends a link to the project through the share button, allowing members to join easily just by clicking on the link.

When participants join the project, each member can work on a different part of a slide or on different slides. A group can build a storyboard or presentation together and brainstorm collaboratively, and when they complete the project, they can save the video to be shared online as a link, or download it in MP4 format. In this way, people who were not able to attend the whiteboard session can still get a sense of the process behind it. Created projects files are also saved to the *Explain Drive* and can be edited anytime. Overall, users can construct group projects on *Explain Everything* (2011) when they are geographically separate from each other.

Explain Everything in a flipped learning classroom

Adopting a flipped classroom model means reversing the delivery of typical elements of the long-established teacher-centered paradigm, seeing students engage with these elements outside of the classroom, at home, and prior to lessons (Roehl, Reddy, & Shannon, 2013). In a flipped teaching model, students first study the class lecture or instructional content by themselves, mostly using video content prepared by instructors, and then apply the knowledge gained from exposure to this content when returning to the classroom and undertaking practical work. One of the benefits of this model is that learners can effectively use the time in class to work through problems, advance concepts, and engage in collaborative learning (Tucker, 2012). It also reverses the role of the teacher from that of a lecturer to that of a coach

(Renard, 2019). Flipped learning is viewed as an example of blended learning as it is a mix of face-to-face interaction in class with online learning elements. When students come to class having already engaged with the topic that is going to be taught, classes can be more engaging and interactive (Bergmann & Sams, 2012). The teacher also already has an expectation of student knowledge levels, and can then focus on areas where students have difficulty with understanding. Overall, flipped learning gives students an increasing responsibility for their own learning, and assists in building learner autonomy.

How one can use Explain Everything for flipped learning?
Instructors can prepare pre-recorded videos of the content that is to be taught for the upcoming class and send it to the students. Here teachers can use *Explain Everything* (2011) to record and screencast the content to make explanatory tutorials and instructional videos before making them available online or by sending it to students for class preparation. Teachers can even record themselves by using the front-facing camera of a supported device, and they do not need to give the same lecture over and over again. Further and foremost, students do not need to worry about losing the key points of the lecture as the video classes sent by their teachers can be stored in the local storage of the device that they are using. Because of its on-demand access, those videos can be used by students to refer back to content, when preparing for exams, and for keeping themselves up-to-speed if they have been absent from class for any reason.

Giving digital descriptive feedback with *Explain Everything*
One of the most import tasks for teachers is providing students with effective feedback that can help them progress forward. Gates (2013) notes, people need others around them who can give them feedback in order to improve. Many educators also claim

how useful feedback can be for motivating and helping students in terms of improving their performance (Wiggins, 2016). For many years, teachers have given feedback on student work in the form of either oral communication in the classroom or written comments on papers handed back to learners, mostly corrected using red pen. Sometimes illegible handwriting or incomprehensible decoding comments, abbreviations and editing terms make it complicated for students to revise corrective feedback given by teachers (Clements, 2006), and therefore, students are likely to feel confused and frustrated when they are unable to find any precise solution that matches with whatever the teacher wants corrected (Thompson & Lee, 2012). Anson (1989) argued that marking what is wrong and right in terms of feedback holds an authoritative tone, which is negatively perceived by learners.

Under the advancement of technology, several alternatives to conventional feedback mechanisms have been explored and with the right technology teachers can deliver more in-depth critique of students' work in a short period of time, and this can lead to feedback that is understood and can be actioned upon, which could lead to greater learning. One of the most used and most effective ways to integrate technology for the delivery of feedback learning is combining text with video or a voice recorder – 'veedback' (Cabot & Levesque, 2015). Thompson & Lee (2012) indicate that students view veedback as the teacher explaining and giving guidance rather than pointing out mistakes. Instructors can use *Explain Everything* (2011) to deliver veedback by both direct video feedback or they can use the screencasting tool. In particular, the following benefits make this whiteboard unique for giving comments.

Timeliness
Although classroom sizes are increasing and workloads are escalating, teachers can easily save time by uploading any

documents or images that need feedback into the canvas of the whiteboard, tapping records or videos, and giving comments. According to Denton (2014), the average person types 30 words per minute but they can speak about 135 words in the same timeframe. As speaking is a faster process, students can receive feedback sooner and teachers can perhaps complete the process in a timelier manner.

Value and clarity
Using visuals, illustrations, screencasts, videos and sound makes the feedback provided via *Explain Everything* (2011) multimodal, which can lead to insightful explanations and suggestions for students' work-in-progress and to fostering metacognitive skills. The pointer tool on the menu bar is what helps the instructor to indicate areas of improvement and to clarify points (e.g., on students' writing). This is useful since Orsmand and Merry (2011) illustrate that students appreciate audio and video commentaries as they are more engaging, personal and easier to understand. Besides this, a teacher's tone, pronunciation, expression and emphasis in terms of conversational feedback makes such comments much more conveying (Middleton, Nortcliffe & Owens, 2009).

Sharing
Focus moves to the delivery of the project after the content has been developed. Simple digital delivery of visual feedback to the target is key. *Explain Everything* videos can be exported directly from the app for delivery to learners via email, a learning management system (LMS), or a cloud-based storage platform.

Ongoing feedback sessions
When the project is shared, the audience can join it, view the feedback and respond to it. Sessions can be conducted synchronously or asynchronously. Synchronous feedback

sessions may give learners a feeling as if they are in the same room with the teacher. Faster narration with screencasting, voice recording and video feedback all enable instructors to not only identify problems, but also provide suggestions concerning improvement (Emery & Atkinson, 2009). Lastly, unlike handwritten feedback, which can be lost or damaged, digitally delivered feedback can be stored on the local storage of students' mobile devices, and it can also be archived by instructors, and thus provides a permanent record (Abrahamson, 2010). As Khan and Joshi (2006) indicate, one of the key factors that easily catches students' attention regarding the quality of e-learning content is its anywhere, anytime accessibility.

How can *Explain Everything* lend itself to TESOL?

Originally, *Explain Everything* (2011) is an educational application that can be used both by teachers and students in multifarious ways both inside and outside of the language learning classroom. The application creates an environment where students can develop as lifelong learners with minimal training on the use of the app.

Explain Everything for EFL/ESL teachers
Delivering classroom instruction

One of the fundamental aspects of effective classroom teaching practice is mastering instruction-giving techniques (Sowell, 2017). Interactive whiteboards can aid in this process as students believe that instruction with an interactive whiteboard has a positive effect on their learning experience owing to increased contextualization and visualization, effectual presentation and the motivational characteristics that the medium can provide in the learning experience (Şad & Özhan, 2012). Inevitably, some classroom activities can be quite complicated in the way that they are organized, especially, when instructions are given in a language other than learners' L1. In this case, not only students but teachers themselves might be likely to get confused as to what to do. Research shows that clear instruction has a direct influence on learning, and the objectives of the class have failed when learners do not understand what they are supposed to do (Sowell, 2017). Using the audio recording, writing, drawing, animating, camera and screencasting tools of *Explain Everything* (2011) can help teachers to highlight important details and steps in the instructional process. Teachers are also able to prepare homework instructions accompanying comprehensible guided tasks so that students are not confused as to what to do and how to do it (e.g., what to read for an assignment and what associated activities to complete).

Preparing tutorial classes
Instructors may choose appropriate 'templates' stemming from the curriculum areas that they are planning to teach when using *Explain Everything* (2011). Becoming aware of students' learning styles and different learning pace, teachers are able to prepare tutorial classes that explain various topics by using techniques such as digital storytelling, and implementing this in instructional videos provided to students prior to class so that learners have engaged with content and understand the notion of what will be taught in class. Instructors may not have enough time to go over the same concept repeatedly as students learn at different speeds. So, providing such content to students also allows them to review basic fundamental concepts in order to master the content of the lesson well. With *Explain Everything* (2011), teachers can archive, and make available, all content they have developed and provide access to it for those who may wish to restudy the topic.

Explain Everything for EFL/ESL learners
Giving (animated) presentations and peer tutoring
Explain Everything (2011) is like giving an interactive whiteboard and a microphone to each student in the classroom. Students can

output their homework assignments in a visual manner with engaging video creations, simple explanations, animations and simple slideshows, and this frees them from paperwork and written worksheets. Students can share the files and projects that they create, which leads to a different approach to assessment over traditional test and paper evaluation methods. Through such projects, teachers may see how well their students have understood the topic. Students can also take on the role of teachers and explain key concepts of a task by creating and sharing their own tutorials. Those students who need any help in that specific area can then access this, teacher reviewed, peer-developed content. Research shows that peer-tutoring has benefits for both tutors and tutees (Darrow, Gibbs, & Wedel, 2005). Because those students who are instructing their peers feel responsible for organizing and clarifying the learning material – all of which assists in their own comprehension of the content.

Redrafting and brainstorming
After teachers have provided online feedback, it is much easier for students to edit their assignments according to the comments given by the teacher. Students can then create digital notebooks for brainstorming by writing notes with the pen tool or the word processor, and dictating notes with the recording feature. They can also consolidate their thoughts on an easily accessible workstation of the interactive whiteboard.

How to start using *Explain Everything* with students

Before starting to use *Explain Everything* (2011) in the classroom, teachers should check whether all students have devices that can use the application so that no one in the class feels left out. The teacher can also tell learners to bring their mobile devices for the upcoming class, and those who are going to use their smartphones or tablet can preinstall the application, and those with laptops can make use of the website. Prior to use of the application for group collaboration, it is much preferable to ensure students have used it for individual projects so that they can become quite familiar with the features, tools and the intricacies of the application. If learners want the project they are going to create on the board to be stored on the *Explain Drive*, they must create an individual account, but this is not required otherwise. With regards to group projects, it is enough for only the group administrator to possess an account. Although the majority of tools available through the application are easy to use, some features like audio editing require the teacher's explanation. At the very beginning, teachers should give a brief introduction to what *Explain Everything* (2011) is and what features and tools learners can make use of. As a tutorial, they can show some short YouTube videos on how to work with the application (e.g., see Elkhart Instructional Technology, 2017). However, it might not be enough for learners and the teacher to show a real process of creating a project on a big screen. It is therefore advisable that the teacher provides an explanation as the students follow allowing by performing the same steps on their own device.

How are students' outputs on *Explain Everything* evaluated?

How effectively the interactive whiteboard is used depends on the imagination of the student or the teacher and the purpose of the class, therefore, instructors should be careful with the process of evaluation. For example, they may wrongly start to assess learners' creativeness and imaginativeness instead of language skills. Teacher feedback and peer feedback may generate better results rather than just grading students' work with relative numbers. An option is to use the application to create an e-portfolio which contains all the artifacts that the students have created, collected and organized within a certain academic period. This kind of digital portfolio can also be a reflective tool to present the growth of learners' skills and knowledge over time (Bala, Mansor, Stapa & Zakaria, 2012).

Obstacles for the lack of use for interactive whiteboards

The findings of research conducted with students and teachers in classroom-based environments in several countries reveal that foreign language teachers are still far from clearly understanding the benefits and limitations of interactive whiteboard technology in language teaching and learning processes (Orr, 2008; Gray, 2010; Mathews-Aydinli & Elaziz, 2010). The fact that the integration of interactive whiteboards is a relatively recent development in language teaching pedagogy, and a lack of specific training on how to use this technology in language teaching classrooms, along with a lack of funding to provide them, might be key factors responsible for lack of use. These obstacles can be overcome providing that teachers as well as students, together with parents, are provided with technical accessibility to Interactive whiteboards by institutions. Adequate training regarding use of the software is another fundamental issue to consider prior to utilizing these tools in the classroom. Moreover, different functions of Interactive whiteboards can be explored by continuously working with them not only during class time, but also after class hours. Armstrong, Barnes, Sutherland, Curran, Mills, & Thompson (2005) indicate that interactive whiteboard use can stimulate new thinking and engage students in interactivity that has the potential, over conventional boards, to lead to greater success. In regards to *Explain Everything* (2011), the cost of both the hardware and the software is relatively affordable. Also, teachers and learners can begin using the application with only a minimal amount of training. Subscribing with the whole class as a team allows users to create an unlimited number of projects.

Conclusion

This chapter has provided a brief overview and exploration into how the interactive whiteboard application called *Explain Everything* (2011) can be used by teachers and students for flipped learning and collaborative learning in a language teaching classroom. Despite the fact that interactive whiteboards like *Explain Everything* (2011) have multimodal features that can engage students with the classroom environment, these devices are not used extensively in foreign language classrooms, and perhaps now with the guidance from this chapter that may change.

References

Abrahamson, E. (2010). Assessment through video-feedback on an undergraduate sports rehabilitation programme. *Higher Education Academy [HEA] Case Study*.

Anson, C. M. (1989). *Writing and Response: Theory, Practice, and Research*. Urbana: National Council of Teachers of English.

Armstrong, V., Barns, S., Sutherland, R., Currans, S., Mills, S., & Thompson, I. (2005). Collaborative research methodology for investigating teaching and learning: The use of interactive whiteboard technology. *Educational Review, 57*(4), 457-469.

Bala, S. S., Mansor, W. F. A. W., Stapa, M., & Zakaria, M. H. (2012). Digital portfolio and professional development of language teachers. *Procedia-Social and Behavioral Sciences, 66*, 176-186. https://doi.org/10.1016/j.sbspro.2012.11.259

Beeland Jr, W. D. (2002). Student engagement, visual learning and technology: Can interactive whiteboards help? *Action Research Exchange, 1*(1). Retrieved from http://citeseerx.ist.psu.edu/viewdoc/download?doi=10.1.1.135.3542&rep=rep1&type=pdf

Beldarrain, Y. (2006). Distance education trends: Integrating new technologies to foster student interaction and collaboration. *Distance education, 27*(2), 139-153.

Bell, M. A. (2002). Why use an interactive whiteboard? A baker's dozen reasons. *The Teacher's Net Gazette, 3*(1).

Bergmann, J., & Sams, A. (2012). *Flip your classroom: Reach every student in every class every day.* USA: International Society for Technology in Education

Bryant, S. M., & Hunton, J. E. (2000). The use of technology in the delivery of instruction: Implications for accounting educators and education researchers. *Issues in Accounting Education, 15*(1), 129-162.

Cabot, I., & Levesque, M. (2015). Audiovisual feedback: Worthwhile practice? *Pedagogie Collegiale, 28*(3), 1-6.

Clements, P. (2006). *Teachers' feedback in context: A longitudinal study of L2 writing classrooms.* (Unpublished doctoral dissertation). University of Washington, USA.

Darrow, A. A., Gibbs, P., & Wedel, S. (2005). Use of classwide peer tutoring in the general music classroom. *Update: Applications of Research in Music Education, 24*(1), 15-26.

Denton, D. (2014, November). Using screen capture feedback to improve academic performance. *TechTrends, 58*(6), 51-56.

Elkhart Instructional Technology. (2017). Explain Everything tutorial. YouTube. Retrieved from https://www.youtube.com/watch?v=aFQOS_MBWPQ

Emery, R., & Atkinson, A. (2009). Group assessment feedback: 'The good, the bad and the ugly'. *A Word in User Ear – Audio Feedback Conference,* December 18. Sheffield, UK. Retrieved from https://research.shu.ac.uk/lti/awordinyourear2009/docs/emery-atkinson-Solent_Audio_Feedback_paper.pdf

Explain Everything. (2011). *Interactive whiteboard application.* New York: Explain Everything.

Explain Everything (2018). About Us. Retrieved from https://explaineverything.com/about

Gates, B. (2013, May 08). Bill Gates: Teachers need real feedback. [Video file]. Retrieved from http://www.youtube.com/watch?v=81Ub0SMxZQo

Glover, D., Miller, D., Averis, D., & Door, V. (2005). The interactive whiteboard: a literature survey. *Technology, Pedagogy and Education, 14*(2), 155-170.

Gray, C. (2010). Meeting teachers' real needs: New tools in the secondary modern foreign languages classroom. In M. Thomas, & E. Schmid (Eds.), *Interactive whiteboards for education: Theory, research and practice* (pp. 69-85). Hershey, PA: IGI Global.

Harasim, L. M., Hiltz, S. R., Teles, L., & Turoff, M. (1995). *Learning networks: A field guide to teaching and learning online.* Cambridge, MA: MIT press.

Henke Jr, J. W., Locander, W. B., Mentzer, J. T., & Nastas III, G. (1988). Teaching techniques for the new marketing instructor: Bringing the business world into the classroom. *Journal of Marketing Education, 10*(1), 1-10.

Herrington, J., Oliver, R., & Reeves, T. C. (2003). Patterns of engagement in authentic online learning environments. Australian Journal of Educational Technology, *19*(1), 59–71.

Herrington, J., Reeves, T. C., Oliver, R., & Woo, Y. (2004). Designing authentic activities in Web-based courses. Journal of Computing in Higher Education, *16*(1), 3–29.

Khan, B. H., & Joshi, V. (2006). E-learning who, what and how? *Journal of Creative Communications, 1*(1), 61-74.

Mathews-Aydinli, J., & Elaziz, F. (2010). Turkish students' and teachers' attitudes toward the use of interactive whiteboards in EFL classrooms. *Computer Assisted Language Learning, 23*(3), 235-252.

Mercier, E., Vourloumi, G., & Higgins, S. (2017). Student interactions and the development of ideas in multi-touch and paper-based collaborative mathematical problem solving. *British Journal of Educational Technology, 48*(1), 162-175.

Middleton, A., Nortcliffe, A., & Owen, R. (2009). iGather: Learners as responsible audio collector of tutor, peer and self reflection. *A Word in User Ear – Audio Feedback Conference*, December 18. Sheffield, UK. Retrieved from http://shura.shu.ac.uk/14444

Orr, M. (2008). Learner perceptions of interactive whiteboards in EFL classrooms. *Call-EJ Online, 9*(2). Retrieved from http://callej.org/journal/9-2/orr.html

Orsmond, P., & Merry, S. (2011, March). Feedback alignment: effective and ineffective links between tutors' and students' understanding of coursework feedback. *Assessment & Evaluation in Higher Education, 36*(2), 125-136.

Peacock, M. (2001). Match or mismatch? Learning styles and teaching styles in EFL. *International Journal of Applied Linguistics, 11*(1), 1-20.

Reid, J. M. (1995). *Learning styles in the ESL/EFL classroom*. Boston, MA: Heinle & Heinle.

Roehl, A., Reddy, S. L., & Shannon, G. J. (2013). The flipped classroom: An opportunity to engage millennial students through active learning strategies. *Journal of Family & Consumer Sciences, 105*(2), 44-49.

Şad, S. N., & Özhan, U. (2012). Honeymoon with IWBs: A qualitative insight in primary students' views on instruction with interactive whiteboard. *Computers & Education, 59*(4), 1184-1191.

Sowell, J. (2017). Good instruction-giving in the second-language classroom. *English Teaching Forum, 55*(3), 10-19.

Thompson, R., & Lee, M. J. (2012). Talking with students through screencasting: Experimentations with video feedback to improve student learning. *The Journal of Interactive Technology and Pedagogy, 1*(1), 1-16

Tucker, B. (2012). The flipped classroom. *Education Next, 12*(1), 82-83.

Warwick, P., & Kershner, R. (2008). Primary teachers' understanding of the interactive whiteboard as a tool for children's collaborative learning and knowledge-building. *Learning, Media and Technology, 33*(4), 269-287.

William, D. (2016). The secret of effective feedback. *Educational Leadership, 73*(7), 10-15.

Wishart, J., & Blease, D. (1999). Theories underlying perceived changes in teaching and learning after installing a computer network in a secondary school. *British Journal of Educational Technology, 30*(1), 25-41.

Appendix A
Lesson Plan

Level of Proficiency and Maturity	English proficiency: intermediate. Age: students from upper elementary school to high school.
Lesson Length	50 minutes.
Lesson Topic	Grammar topic: Present Participle.
Objectives	To consolidate students' comprehension of the different uses of the present participle integrating the *Explain Everything* interactive whiteboard.
Outcomes	Students will be able to use the present participle both as adjectives and in continuous verb tenses in authentic contexts.
Relevant Prior Learning	The present participle has to have been explained during previous classes, with the current class being devoted only to strengthening the learners' comprehension of the topic by applying the grammar to potentially real-life contexts. Besides that, *Explain Everything* should be introduced prior to this class. Students should have some idea of the features and tools that exist regarding the interactive whiteboard they will use during the class.

Teacher Preparation	
Hardware	Both the teacher and each student in the class need to have a mobile device in order to see video and be able to create a project on the interactive whiteboard. Other equipment that is required for the class is a laptop, a projector, whiteboard, and speakers.
Software	The *Explain Everything* application.
Webpage Links	If there are any students who are unaware of how to use *Explain Everything*, below is a link for a six-minute tutorial that introduces *Explain Everything*: https://www.youtube.com/watch?v=aFQOS_MBWPQ The following links are sample projects prepared by the teacher to show students so that they can have a clear idea of what to do as a class assignment: - https://expl.ai/CQQJXLT - https://expl.ai/MDVQTBE - https://expl.ai/LHQTVDY
Additional Resources	Present Participle handout (see Appendix B).

Procedure			
Stage and Timing	Objective	Teacher	Students
Review Stage **(7 minutes)**	1. Revise the grammar point (present participle) that was explained in the previous class. 2. Briefly review how to use *Explain Everything*, what tools exist, and what features it has.	1. Ask what students remember about the previously-explained topic, and distribute the handout (Appendix B). 2. Show a short video (webpage link 1) on the use of *Explain Everything* to students, and practice it on a real whiteboard. 3. Answer learners' questions. 4. Check whether all students in the class own any mobile device and have installed the *Explain Everything* application.	1. Share what they remember on the present participle. 2. Ask for more clarification if there are any questions or misunderstandings on the grammar topic or the use of the interactive whiteboard. 3. Make sure that you have installed the *Explain Everything* app if using a smartphone or tablet for the class activity.

Warm-up Stage/Pre-Technology Use (8 minutes)	Explain the activity and how to do it.	Give instructions and guidance on how to perform the activity, and provide some samples (webpage links: 2, 3, 4) so that students have a clear idea about what to do and how to do it.	Listen to the teacher's instructions and view the sample projects.
Main Stage/Technology-based Activity (10 minutes)	Allow students to relate the concepts and language content that is introduced in the lesson to an authentic context, and one that is conducted outside of the classroom.	Allow students to go out of the classroom and to film short videos regarding actions that they need to perform in order to carry out their projects.	Go out and film about 10 short videos of actions on the process so that they can relate these to the present participle later (e.g., People walking, a child crying, a friend taking a photograph).

Practice Stage (15 minutes)	Allow students to utilize the *Explain Everything* interactive whiteboard application to become familiar with it in a practical way and to apply the skills and knowledge that they acquired during the lesson.	1. Give instructions to students to make their own short projects focusing on the use of the present participle. 2. Walk around the class and see how the students are doing. If anyone has difficulty with the use of the technology, help them.	1. They return to the class and create their own projects, uploading the short videos they have taken to the *Explain Everything* canvas. 2. Using their imagination they make example sentences using the present participle. For example, they have a 10-secund video of people walking. They upload it to the canvas and make the sentence '*I saw people walking.*' According to their English proficiency level and creativeness, they can make up some complex sentences and design them using the interactive whiteboard using audio, screencasting, and graphic editing tools.

Lesson Summation Stage/Post-Technology Activities (10 minutes)	1. The instructor reinforces the importance of language concepts and skills in real-life contexts. 2. The instructor elicits students' opinion on the effectiveness of technology integration in the class.	1. Ask students to complete and summarize their work and make presentations of what they have created, these can then be shared with the class. 2. Ask how useful the students have found *Explain Everything*, and what difficulties they encountered.	1. Complete the activity and make a presentation. 2. Share opinions about the process of working with *Explain Everything*, the benefits of it, and the difficulties experienced while working with it.

	Further Considerations
Contingency Plan(s)	Sometimes there can be unexpected problems that might hinder the class in terms of following the plan that the teacher has prepared in advance. In the case of the above class, not all students may have mobile devices to use, which might make some students feel disappointed. In that case, the teacher can ask students in other classes to lend their gadgets for the fifty-minute class.
Evaluation	Students will have great interest in how they can use *Explain Everything* at the beginning of the class. As part of the class is held in an authentic context, students will be able to realize how language learning is related to their everyday lives, which is far more likely to encourage them to be actively engaged in the language learning process. Best of all, technology integration into the class as a primary factor can be attractive for 'digital natives,' even passive learners, and engage them with the activity. However, if it is the students' first attempt to make use of *Explain Everything*, they may have some difficulties with audio and video editing. The opinions that the students share at the end of the class about the advantages and difficulties that they have with the use of *Explain Everything* can be analyzed by the teacher. It can help for assisting the teacher in developing better lessons, and for further improvement in terms of using application, and interactive whiteboards with classes.

Appendix B
The Use of the Present Participle

The present participle as part of the continuous form of a verb:
- My mother is cooking.
- I was cleaning my room.

The present participle after verbs of movement and position:
- Unfortunately, I could not go camping with my friends last week.
- I am planning to go cycling this weekend.

The present participle after verbs of perception:
- I overheard them talking about the final exam.
- I saw a little child crying along the street.

The present participle as an adjective:
- Students can find some learning materials in the library.
- There is an increasing demand for electronic devices.

The present participle for nouns of activity:
- Many people think that reading a lot is a key factor for success.
- I prefer staying at home to going out in rainy weather.

The present participle with the verbs *spend* and *waste*:
- My friend wasted his time being unemployed for a long time.
- She spent all her money buying clothes that she does not need.

The present participle with the verbs *catch* and *find*:
- The children have been caught stealing some jewelry.
- I found my sister sitting in the dark room.

The present participle for two actions at the same time:
- I used to do my assignments listening to music and it distracted me a lot.
- After graduating from university, he found a job in a Korean company.

The present participle to explain a reason:
- Being an active student, she participated in all group projects in the class.
- Running out of money, Ann called me to ask about debt.

6. Language Teaching and Technology: A Less-is-More Approach to Integration in the Classroom

Natasha Reddy
TESOL-MALL Graduate Program, Woosong University

Introduction

In considering the concept of 'fit-for-purpose' as it relates to the use of digital technologies in language learning, the primary aim of this chapter is to show that, while there is an amazingly diverse range of technologies and applications that are available for use in language learning, more is not automatically better. It is suggested that classroom practice is better served by using one or two familiar platforms instead of multiple platforms. To this end, the use of the Kakao Corporation (Kakao, 2010) *KakaoTalk* application as a tool to help develop listening, speaking, reading and writing in the English as a foreign language (EFL) context of the Republic of Korea is explored, along with options for the use of *KakaoTalk* across different teaching and learning approaches – whether teacher- or student-centered. We conclude that encouraging more focused and creative use of existing technologies is better than adding more diverse technologies to the language classroom.

Language Teaching and Technology: A Less-is-More Approach to Integration in the Classroom

The Fourth Industrial Revolution, while building on the Third, is distinctly different in that it is marked by rapid advancements in technology and science (Xu, David & Kim, 2018), and these are advancements that are disrupting and changing human-to-human interactions, human- to-machine interactions and machine- to-machine interactions. Klaus Schwab (as cited in Xu et al., 2018), who coined the term 'Fourth Industrial Revolution,' indicated that it is marked by the fusing and blurring of boundaries between the physical, digital and biological spheres. This is the new era of interconnectedness of people and machines. This interconnectedness, as exemplified by mobile digital technology, brings with it a reconceptualizing of what constitutes 'work,' 'leisure', and 'learning,' creating a new scenario where all three aspects can be done anywhere and at any time (Kadyte, 2003). This new framework comes with different opportunities for, and challenges to, the field of education. Teachers are being challenged, more than ever, to utilize new technologies to engage and stimulate their students in the classroom, whilst those self-same students engage in increasingly complex digital practices outside the classroom (Knobel & Kalman, 2016). Teachers now have access to an amazingly diverse range of technologies and applications that are meant to 'assist' them in achieving best practice within their teaching/learning contexts. Yet are these technologies all fit-for-purpose? In other words, do the technologies and applications (hereafter, apps) fit the needs of EFL students and teachers alike?

In the context of EFL instruction in the Republic of Korea (hereafter Korea), this chapter answers the following questions:

1. Can digital tools and mobile assisted language learning (MALL) enable better learning for EFL students?
2. Are digital tools and MALL used consistently in the EFL classroom practice?
3. What criteria should guide the choice of digital tools in the EFL classroom?
4. Are the tools chosen 'fit-for-purpose'?

Literature Review

The integration of technology into the EFL classroom is by no means a new concept. Many researchers have examined the potential and practical uses of computers and technology in the language classroom (Allen & Tanner, 2006; Brady, Holcomb &

Smith, 2010; Carini, Kuh, & Klein, 2006; Warschauer, 2000; Zheng, Yim & Warschauer, 2017). The use of computer-assisted language learning (CALL), computer-assisted classroom discussion (CACD), and MALL provide enhanced opportunities for students to not only interact and engage in a wider social forum, but also expands opportunities for participation, collaboration, and self-expression (Kessler, 2013; Kikuchi & Otsuka,2008). Technology, therefore, is not just a potential tool *in* learning, but it is also a catalyst *for* learning (McLoughlin & Oliver, 2002).

EFL instruction in particular has benefited from accessing those literacy activities that students may already be engaged in and using them within the classroom context (Zheng, et al., 2017). Gaming, emailing, texting/chatting, maintaining online profiles, publishing/posting, and other literacy-rich activities have been used for pedagogical purposes, and the added benefit for an ESL classroom is that these activities have social and personal relevance and importance for the individual student, and as such, carry greater motivation than would print/classroom-based activities. There has also been significant research on the benefit of social networking sites (SNSs), such as Facebook, Twitter and *KakaoTalk*, for EFL learning (Alnujaidi, 2017; Barrot, 2016; Schreiber, 2015; Yen, Hou, & Chang, 2015; Yunus, Salehi, & Chenzi, 2012). Research then seems to support the view that the use of MALL with digital technologies, such as SNSs, has the potential to benefit EFL students' learning by improving student motivation, involvement, and engagement as well as serving the very specific needs of students in different fields of study (Allen & Tanner, 2006; Carini, et al., 2006; Chewon & Jin, 2015; Heafner, 2004).

However, while research indicates that there is a benefit in *using* technology in the EFL classroom, the actual reality of technology integration in the EFL classroom seems to be different (Flanagan & Shoffner, 2013; Sherman, 2016; Tour, 2015). There is a range of factors that have been identified as creating 'barriers' to teachers who are integrating technology into their teaching. Some of the factors linked to these barriers are systemic (to do with access and institutional requirements), psychological (personal mindsets, personal use of and experience with technology, and confidence and understanding of technological requirements), and social/professional (beliefs regarding pedagogical usefulness, insufficient training/teaching experience, lack of awareness of pedagogical approaches, and time constraints for preparation and administration) (Sherman, 2016; Tour, 2015).

While a full examination of teachers' attitudes, perceptions, and use of technology is beyond the scope of this paper, the point of view being presented here is that having more technology and digital tools has not changed the levels of use and integration in classrooms. To address this discrepancy, the suggestion here is that classroom practice can be better served by teachers choosing one or two highly versatile digital tools instead of having to navigate numerous different apps. To navigate the dynamic of the barriers listed above, and to ensure that the tool helps meet the objectives of EFL, the main criteria for selection would be that it

1. is readily accessible to students and teachers alike,
2. does not require extensive orientation and therefore is easy to master, and
3. provides an authentic part of the students' and teachers' day-to-day technology use.

To this end, *KakaoTalk* is proposed as being the ideal digital tool for MALL in the Korean context.

What is *KakaoTalk*?

KakaoTalk is a free, mobile instant messaging app with chat (text, video, images, and emoticons) and call (voice and video) features. Launched on March 18, 2010 and currently available on iOS, Android, Bada OS, BlackBerry, Windows Phone, Nokia Asha, Windows, and MacOS, the app allows for 1:1 and group interactions and has a range of additional features, for example, boards which allow for announcements, photo/video/file/link sharing, event notifications and a poll feature. The use of QR codes as identity recognition, paying for services and goods, ordering food, gaming and sharing of games, music, in-chat browser search functionality, and location-specific services means that *KakaoTalk* extends beyond just a chat or messenger app, making it the most popular messenger app in Korea with a rapidly growing user-base globally.

How can I use *KakaoTalk*?
KakaoTalk uses a Kakao account and does not require a cellphone number to be activated. One can simply download the app from Google Play, the App Store, or the Microsoft Store. *KakaoTalk* can be used on smartphones, Apple iPads, and personal computers (PCs), and once installed, it is a simple matter of creating a profile and becoming familiar with the range of features. A few features which make this a better choice for classroom use is 'Plus Friend' and the 'Quick Response (QR) contact reader'. These features enable seemingly effortless creation of group chats, and there is no need for sending/receiving individual contact details. Rather, the group creator can simply scan each member's QR code or conduct a quick search for contacts using the app (you only need a user/contact name instead of their cell number) and invite them to join the group chat. Use of the app requires a wifi connection but is generally much more cost effective than similar messenger services.

What types of *KakaoTalk* exist?
While this paper presents *KakaoTalk* as a good tool for the EFL class, the intention is to suggest the use of similar types of apps as being fit for the purpose of language instruction. Similar apps include WeChat (China), Line (Japan), WhatsApp (India, Europe, Africa) and Facebook Messenger (North America, Africa,

Europe). While these are not the only messenger service apps available, they are indicated as being the most popular according to region (Clement, 2019). All these apps have the core functionality of text, voice chat, and multimedia sharing, and they could easily be integrated into EFL learning. One of the key factors to consider with messenger apps is the ease of access and cost. Messenger apps often allow for free chats (text and video), and this is particularly important in terms of wanting students to have access to MALL tools. Korea, with an internet penetration rate of 96% (Poushter, Bishop & Chwe, 2018) is well suited to the use of MALL without significant impact to students' access. Other countries, however, are not the same, with South Africa, for example, still facing challenges in terms of internet access and data costs, so while teachers and students in certain areas may have access to a smartphone, they are still restricted in the apps/tools they can access, afford, or use. Messenger apps (in the case of South Africa, WhatsApp) present themselves as 'equal opportunity' tools that will be familiar to both teachers and students (Gulati, 2008).

What elements are behind an effective *KakaoTalk* lesson/integration?

The key aspect of using *KakaoTalk* and other messenger apps is the element of authenticity where the student engages with the app as a natural part of their day-to-day routine and not for the distinct purpose of learning. Also, for the use of *KakaoTalk* to be successful, there must be creativity in how it is integrated. Kim and Yoon (2014), in their examination of the use of *KakaoTalk* and *Mobile café (Mocafé)* in the EFL writing class, identify the need for "well-organized blending … for successful language learning" (p.86). A key element that should be remembered when planning *KakaoTalk* lessons is that the app should not become just a place to post homework, or a drill using a question/answer format. The app has a wide range of functionality to create engaging lessons

– video, media, voice, images, games, etc. – which can all be added into a lesson with minimal effort. Lastly, to be effective, there must be consistency in the use of the app, both in providing ESL learning and practice opportunities and in providing timely feedback to students. Using the app as a novelty, once-off, or simply to be experimental is sure to cause students to lose interest.

How can *KakaoTalk* lend itself to teaching English to speakers of other languages (TESOL)?

KakaoTalk lends itself to TESOL primarily because of accessibility and authenticity, and it is a ready-made platform for language sharing, expression, and meaning-making. It is SNS- compressed and user-friendly, and unlike SNS platforms such as Facebook and Twitter, where one can have an account but not engage in any meaningful way (passive observer and consumer of others' posts, newsfeeds, and so on), messenger apps *require* a response. Whether it is an emoticon, sticker, gif, text message, video, or voice note, 'text etiquette' requires a response. For TESOL, the benefit is that students engage with the material, generate their own content to express meaning – in whatever form that content may be. The wide range of features in *KakaoTalk* enable its use for a range of different educational purposes, and in the context of EFL, *KakaoTalk* can be used to engage students in writing activities via texting. The voice note feature allows for speaking practice, and by sharing media and files, the areas of listening and reading are engaged. The polling feature is interesting in that, with a bit of planning and creative thought, it could be used as a quiz. The link sharing feature also enables you to simply share resources and activities created in other apps. For example, if using *KakaoTalk* to initiate discussion and debate (spoken or written), you can link various videos, audio files, or articles directly in the chat. Access to educational programs, for example, bookwidgets

(Kidimedia, 2019) which allows you to create teaching and learning resources, is as simple as sharing a link.

How do I craft a *KakaoTalk* lesson?

If choosing to use *KakaoTalk*, the formulation of materials and content that encourages *meaningful* and authentic engagement would be an essential part of the successful use of the platform. Use of the app would be most effective as part of a blended-learning approach using both offline (classroom) interactions and online interactions (Kim & Yoon, 2014). The following is an explanation of how this approach was used to provide language speaking practice with a university EFL sophomore class. The class ranked as low-intermediate according to university level tests, and consisted of twelve occupational therapy students – ten female, two male. While the students are attentive during the class, getting them to engage and speak freely was challenging. They completed written tasks quite quickly but were more reluctant with pair/group discussions. The course had a listening/speaking focus and used the Cambridge Prism Listening and Speaking Level 3 course book (Lansford & Lockwood, 2017). The classroom interaction (offline) component included teaching and language practice. Students were exposed to the language conventions for stating preferences ('I would rather...', 'I prefer...') and for offering suggestions ('In my opinion...', 'I think that...', 'I would suggest...'). They worked through written and oral activities from the Cambridge Prism textbook (Lansford & Lockwood, 2017, p. 45) in class. In the week following the classroom practice, students were sent a voice note via the *KakaoTalk* class group chat, asking them to state their preference of snacks (cookies or chocolates). The voice-notes were not scheduled, i.e., students were not told when to expect them. The reasoning behind this is to provide a more authentic/real-world situation requiring them to use their English language skills. The voice note feature was used to provide the listening and speaking practice needed for the course. Students were encouraged to frame their verbal responses using the language conventions learned and practiced in class.

The second *KakaoTalk* group chat was initiated by a request for suggestions/advice on the best place to experience the cherry blossoms in Korea. The method of implementation followed the first example, that is, classroom/textbook teaching and practice followed by unscheduled voice-note questions via *KakaoTalk*.

Initially some students were very anxious and requested that they send their responses to the teacher's personal chat as opposed to the group chat. While this request was granted, none of the students used it – they all responded using voice-note in the class group chat. As expected, the responses were very concise but demonstrated the students' ability to use the grammar structures covered in class in a different context. Interestingly, it was noted that students did not respond simply to complete the task but took the initiative to attach media (event information) that corresponded with their verbal suggestions. Also, the dynamic of the group chat created a type of 'peer-pressure' in that once one student added extra information and media, several others followed suit. This speaks to the positive feedback that can occur within online communities, encouraging students to express themselves more confidently than they would in class. There was also an overall increase in the length of the verbal responses. The initial responses ranged from 5 to 10 seconds for the first chat, to 14 to 20 seconds for the later chats. This was in keeping with the nature of the requests.

Overall, the use of *KakaoTalk* allowed for the students to use the language structures taught in class in an authentic manner.

How can I start using *KakaoTalk* with students?

The use of *KakaoTalk* does not require extensive retraining or learning of new technology on the part of the instructor. Neither does it require that the students or the instructor set up additional

SNS accounts or to register and download new apps if they already have it installed and are using it. It proved to be as simple as setting up a class group chat, which was done in less than two minutes amongst thirteen users in class. What is needed, though, is a defining of expectations. Cho (2009) found that failure to discuss expectations and protocols around the use of SNSs led to frustration on the part of the students and disappointment on the part of the instructor. Students should also be assured that this aspect of their SNS use – for exploring and practicing their L2 identity – has a broader benefit beyond getting good grades for homework and participation. It may be necessary for the teacher to keep to an initial schedule, and to give the students an idea of what to expect during the week. This can generally change as students become more confident, at which point the focus can shift from teacher-initiated to student-initiated and directed.

How to evaluate a *KakaoTalk* lesson?

KakaoTalk lessons can be as simple as indicating 'done/not done'; use of checklists (listing course objectives/aims, listing task objectives/goals, or self-checklists for students to use); and determining the number of comments, posts (quantity on online interactions), and rubrics (quality of online interactions). Allen & Tanner (2006) present helpful tools for creating and using rubrics for specific classroom activities, and Kim and Yoon (2014) outline systems that they used to motivate, evaluate, and reward elementary and middle school students in their use of *KakaoTalk* and *Mocafé* in their EFL class. Ultimately, the form of assessment used would reflect the purpose for which *KakaoTalk* is used. As indicated previously, the polling feature on *KakaoTalk* could easily be adapted as a quiz – allowing a teacher to use this to check comprehension/recall along a more traditional format if required. Regarding the examples indicated in this paper, the prescribed rubrics assigned for the course were used, and there was no need to generate new assessment tools.

Conclusion

The main aim of this chapter is to show that the use of familiar, easily accessible tools such as *KakaoTalk* or other messaging apps is not only beneficial for EFL learning but also for EFL teaching. The issues of teachers becoming technology integrators and adapters in their classrooms is more likely to occur if they start with what they already know. The suggestion here is that it is not the number of tools and apps used in the EFL class that will make a difference, but authentic, meaningful and consistent use of whatever technology is preferred by both students and teachers. *KakaoTalk* has been presented as an option for MALL in Korea because it is feature-rich yet simple to use, and it is already a part of the digital toolkit of teachers and students. The simplified approach for teaching and learning presented in this chapter is also easily transferable to other language learning contexts globally. However, this chapter is in no way suggesting that any specific tools be gotten rid of, or that one tool be should used *exclusively*; simply that, when it comes to the teaching of English to speakers of other languages, *more* apps may not always be better.

References

Allen, D., & Tanner, K. D. (2006). Rubrics: Tools for making learning goals and evaluation criteria explicit for both teachers and learners. *CBE-Life Sciences Education, 5*(3), 197-203.

Alnujaidi, S. (2017). Social network sites as ESL/EFL learning and teaching tools: A critical review. *International Journal of Applied Linguistics and English Literature, 6*(3), 34-42.

Barrot, J. S. (2016). Using Facebook-based e-portfolio in ESL writing classrooms: Impact and challenges. *Language, Culture and Curriculum, 29*(3), 286–301.

Brady, K. P., Holcomb, L., & Smith, B. (2010). The use of alternative social networking sites in higher educational settings: A case study of the e-learning benefits of ning in education. *Journal of Interactive Online Learning, 9*(2), 151-170.

Carini, R. M., Kuh, G. D., & Klein, S. P. (2006). student engagement and student learning: Testing the linkages. *Research in Higher Education, 47*(1), 1-32.

Chewon, L., & Jin, H. L. (2015). The effect of task modality and type on Korean EFL learners' interactions. *The Journal of Asia TEFL, 12*(2), 87-123.

Cho, Y. (2009). Investigating the use of social networking site in an ESL writing class. *Multimedia Assisted Language Learning, 12*(3), 9–37.

Clement, J. (2019). Most popular mobile messaging apps worldwide as of April 2019, based on the number of monthly active users (in millions). Statista. Retrieved from https://www.statista.com/statistics/258749/most-popular-global-mobile-messenger-apps

Flanagan, S., Shoffner, M. (2013). Teaching with(out) technology: Secondary English teachers and classroom technology use. *Contemporary Issues in Technology and Teacher Education, 13*(3), 242-261.

Gulati, S. (2008). Technology-enhanced learning in developing nations: A review. *The International Review of Research in Open and Distributed Learning, 9*(1), 1-16.

Heafner, T. L. (2004). Using technology to motivate students to learn social studies. *Contemporary Issues in Technology and Teacher Education, 4*(1), 42-53.

Kakao. (2010). *KakaoTalk*. Seoul: Kakao Corporation.

Kessler, G., (2013). Teaching ESL/EFL in a world of social media, mash-ups, and hyper-collaboration. *TESOL Journal, 4*(4), 615-632.

Kidimedia (2019). *Bookwidgets*. Belgium: Kidimedia.

Kikuchi, K. (2008). Investigating the use of social networking services in Japanese EFL classrooms. *The JALT CALL Journal*, 4(1), 40-52.

Kim. H., & Yoon, M. (2014). Adopting smartphone-based blended learning: An experimental study of the implementation of KakaoTalk and Mocafe. *Multimedia-Assisted Language Learning*, 17(2), 86-111.

Knobel, M., & Kalman, J. (2016). New literacies and teacher learning: Professional development and the digital turn. USA: Peter Lang.

Lansford, L., & Lockwood, R. (2017). *Cambridge Prism Listening and Speaking Level 3*. Cambridge: Cambridge University Press.

McLoughlin, C., & Oliver, R. (2002). Maximizing the language and learning link in computer learning environments. *British Journal of Education Technology*, 29(2), https://doi.org/10.1111/1467-8535.00054

Poushter. J., Bishop, C. & Chwe, H. (2018, June 19). Social media use continues to rise in developing countries but plateaus across developed ones. The Pew Research Center. Retrieved from https://www.pewresearch.org/global/2018/06/19/social-media-use-continues-to-rise-in-developing-countries-but-plateaus-across-developed-ones

Schreiber, B. R. (2015). "I Am What I Am": Multilingual identity and digital translanguaging. Language Learning. *Language Learning and Technology*, 19(3), 69-87.

Sherman, B. J. (2016). *Agency, Ideology, and Information/Communication Technology: English Language Instructor use of Instructional Technology at a South Korean College* (unpublished dissertation). Pennsylvania State University, USA.

Tour, E. (2015). Digital mindsets: Teachers' technology use in personal life and teaching. *Language Learning and Technology*, 19(3), 124-139.

Yen, Y. C., Hou, H. T., & Chang, K. E. (2015). Applying role-playing strategy to enhance learners' writing and speaking skills in EFL courses using Facebook and Skype as learning tools: A case study in Taiwan. *Computer Assisted Language Learning, 28*(5), 383–406, https://doi.org/10.1080/09588221.2013.839568

Yunus, M. M., Salehi, H., & Chenzi, C. (2012). Integrating social networking tools into ESL writing classroom: Strengths and weaknesses. *English Language Teaching, 5*(8), 42.

Zheng, B., Yim, S., & Warschauer, M. (2017). Social Media in the writing classroom and beyond. In J. I. Liontas, (Ed.), *The TESOL Encyclopedia of English Language Teaching* (pp. 1–5). Hoboken, NJ, USA: John Wiley & Sons, Inc.

7. Instructor Preference of Cloud-Based Platform and Quiz Type for Formative Assessment

Irada Gezalova
TESOL-MALL Gradaute Program, Woosong University

Teachers have different preferences for cloud-based platforms when conducting formative assessment, along with the question-types that they provide to learners. As such, the research conducted in this chapter examines the results of a survey that was created in order to understand teachers' tastes relating to question types, their satisfaction rates with cloud-based formative assessment platforms, and the preference of platform use. Based on these results, a cloud-based assessment delivery platform was then chosen for use in the research, and two quizzes with similar tasks but different question types were then provided to participants, namely: a multiple-choice and short-answer quiz via the Google Forms platform. Descriptive analysis was then undertaken regarding the performance of learners utilizing these question-types. Interpretation of these results determines that the most effective quiz type, in terms of obtaining higher scores during formative assessment, is the multiple-choice question type. Ultimately, it is found that Google Forms proves to be a convenient tool for conducting formative assessment, and that student performance on quiz type mostly depends on the content, question types, and the teacher's skills in creating the quiz.

Introduction

The start of the 21st century has been set apart by innovative advancements in how we impart and comprehend data (Fischer & Konomi, 2005). This has led to a growing number of technology-enhanced classrooms and courses, and ones that

Note: The author wishes to thank Gulnoza Sobirova for assistance in data collection.

require consequent modification to the process of assessment, especially since assessment is an integral component of course design. However, conventional paper-and-pencil methods for teaching are still widely used. As Vosylis states (2012), "Collecting research data through traditional paper-and-pencil methods can be costly and time-consuming. This becomes extremely difficult in longitudinal studies ..." (p. 8). The alternative for the traditional paper-and-pencil method is conducting internet-based surveys that are widely used and have the potential (Yun & Trumbo, 2000) to collect, analyze and store a large amount of data. When collecting test results digitally, it is also important to be able to dissect the data in order to follow student advancement and to propose techniques to learners for their development, and this can effectively be achieved by providing opportunities for students to learn from their errors in unobtrusive ways (Watt, 2002). Cloud-based technologies allow data to be stored and processed on the internet, therefore enabling instant data access all over the globe, and therefore can be successfully used in education. Google Forms, as a part of a Google Drive cloud-based office suite, allows for the creation and administering of multiple types of web-based surveys and quizzes, and therefore it can be used to facilitate the process of formative assessment.

Purpose and rationale
Nowadays, a variety of digital tools can be used for formative assessment, such as Google Forms, which provides a variety of question types (checkboxes, checkbox grid, dropdown, linear scale, multiple-choice, multiple-choice grid, paragraph, and short-answer). Knowing which question type to use may lead to possible confusion among educators in regards to selecting the one that will see students perform better during formative assessment. Educators may also be confused with the many types of question-types available, and which may prove to be the better choice for their learning and teaching context. As such, this

research aims to reveal teachers' tastes in choosing quiz question types for digitally delivered formative assessment, and to see how students' responses correlate with the top two question types that instructors tend to employ. To achieve this, the research will rely upon Google Forms, which is free, user-friendly, and easily accessible, and data can be transferred to the Google Sheet spreadsheets application for further analysis (Hallur, 2016). Because Google Forms supports various types of questions, it was selected in order to determine the teachers' overall preference for the formative assessment quiz type and the resulting students' output. In terms of this, the study aims to addresses the following questions:

1. What are the teacher preferences in question types for formative assessment when using Google Forms?
2. Which one is the most effective quiz type in terms of obtaining higher scores during formative assessment?

Literature Review
Assessment

A common problem that often occurs for teachers at universities is the difficulty in organizing student assessment tasks effectively and efficiently (Napitupulu, et al., 2018), with the conventional assessment process based on completing paperwork, which can be a tiresome and sometimes erratic task to achieve. Gathering statistical data and performing analyses of students' preferences regarding assessment can also be difficult and when conducting paper-based tests, which is mostly performed manually it can be very time-consuming (Vosylis, 2012).

Clay (2001) states that there is also an issue with providing formal training in developing tests, adding that forty eight percent of educators have no formal training in test administration, development, scoring or interpretation. As Wright, Aquilino and Supple (1998) note, surveys conducted over the internet are more accurate than surveys that are paper-and-pencil collected, with both data collection and analysis automated and faster. So today, like Scrivener (2011) states,

> The 21st Century teacher needs to take the time to be comfortable with the technological tools that are useful for her students. It's no longer acceptable to write off their use with excuses such as 'I'm not technical' or 'It's not real teaching' (p. 335).

Nowadays, digital literacy plays an important role in education, and many teachers have found that cloud-based technologies can be successfully employed in their classes. One such technology is that of Google Forms, which is a part of the Google Docs platform. The convenience and practical focus of this tool for practitioners has been emphasized by Hallur (2016, p. 1): "Google Form reduces workload, increases efficiency and accuracy of a teacher's work." As an additional function, Google Forms supports multiple templates (e.g., the 'Blank quiz', 'Exit ticket', 'Assessment', 'Worksheet', and 'Course evaluation'). These can all be applied when developing question types, along with answer options using options including: checkboxes, checkbox grid, dropdown, Likert-type scales, multiple-choice, multiple-choice grid, paragraph, or short-answer. Of note, "Google Form includes short response and multiple-choice question types, but only multiple-choice questions provide synchronous feedback data" (Castro, 2018, p. 5).

Methods

This study is based on the quantitative methodology of research, involving survey and test data analysis. Studies using a mixed approach like this one are useful as they can examine quantitative data, relying upon statistical and mathematical techniques when investigating observable phenomena (Lisa, 2008), and they rely upon survey research to "discover relative incidence, distribution, and interrelations" among populations (Kerlinger & Fred, 1973, p. 410).

Ultimately, the survey utilized with teachers was deployed in order to collect data concerning which of two quiz types teachers rely upon the most when creating quizzes for delivery through the Google Forms platform, and to then distribute to student participants quizzes developed using these two quiz types in order to determine which leads to higher accuracy in terms of responses. Completion of the two quizzes by students allowed for the collected data to be descriptively analyzed and presented using the statistical tools incorporated within Google Forms. Further, for these quizzes, students' feedback was not available, therefore student satisfaction cannot be assessed, therefore conclusions will be based upon statistical data, taking into account average points, median points, and range points. Average points here refer to the mean statistical value, which can be calculated just by summing up all values and dividing them by the sample number. This value, known as the statistical mean or average (Godino & Batanero, 2002), can be used to describe the central tendency of the analyzed dataset. Then, in order to avoid skewed average values, the statistical median can be used because it is more tolerant of outliers (Rousseeuw, 1991). The median basically finds one specific value in the dataset, where 50% of the values are bigger than the median, and 50% of the values are smaller than the median number. It better represents the most typical values in the distribution, in comparison with the average value (Rousseeuw, 1991).

Participants
A total of fifty participants were involved in this study, all a sample of convenience (Fraenkel, Wallen & Hyun, 2012). The population sample can be broken down into two groups: thirty teachers and twenty students.

Teachers

Thirty people from two different institutions, a university in Daejeon (South Korea) and an academic lyceum in Samarkand (Uzbekistan), participated in this study. Participants ranged from associate professors to graduate pre-service and in-service teachers (see Table 1), and they were chosen in order to obtain representative answers relying upon their teaching and delivery of online formative assessment to students.

Table 1. *Occupation of teacher participants*

Occupation	Participation Rate	
	N	%
Assistant professors	7	23.3%
Educators	3	10%
Engineering	1	3.3%
English teachers	11	36.7%
Professors	5	16.7%
Student teachers	3	10%
TOTAL	*30*	*100%*

In general, the surveyed teachers' occupations are English teachers, assistant professors, and professors. Teachers reported that they mainly taught subjects related to the English language 36.7% ($n=11$), education 23.3% ($n=7$), business 16.7% ($n=5$), engineering 10% ($n=3$), technology 10% ($n=3$) and one outlier, who reports that he/she has no relevant experience in making quizzes and teaching, as is shown in Table 2.

Students

Twenty students of the English language from an academic lyceum in Samarkand (Uzbekistan) were selected to participate in this study. The population of students was quite uniform; their English skill level is that of intermediate, with the age of all students sixteen (see Table 3).

Table 2. *Subjects taught by teacher participants*

Subjects	Participation Rate	
	n	%
Business	5	16.7%
Education (general)	7	23.3%
Engineering	3	10%
English language	11	36.7%
Technology	3	10%
n/a	1	3.3%
TOTAL	*30*	*100%*

Table 3. *Student profile*

Age		
Years old	Participation Rate	
	n	%
16	20	100
TOTAL	*20*	*100*

English Ability		
Level	Participation Rate	
	n	%
Basic	19	95
Intermediate	1	5
TOTAL	*20*	*100*

Major		
Specialty	Participation Rate	
	n	%
Foreign philology	20	100
TOTAL	*20*	*100*

Instruments

Two instruments were developed for this research study: a survey delivered to educators, and two different quiz types that were developed based on the survey results and delivered to student participants.

Survey

In order to understand teachers' question-type preferences, the conducted survey includes questions regarding teacher demographics (occupation and subjects taught, detailed under participants), and was deployed in order to determine the questions types that these teachers typically employ for formative assessment, the cloud-based platforms that they use to deliver formative assessment to students, and their satisfaction with these platforms.

Quiz types

Survey data of teachers came to highlight multiple-choice and short-answer as the two most popular quiz types delivered by teachers for formative assessment, and as such, these quiz types were used as the basis of obtaining data from the student participants in the study. Both quiz types were developed using vocabulary from Nation (2018) and were designed based on the same lexical teaching material, however, the response format for each quiz differs: multiple-choice and short-answer. The number of questions is the same in each quiz – fifteen questions sharing similar vocabulary topics. The range of a possible quiz score is from zero points up to the maximum value of 75.

Both quizzes were provided to participants via a web link, with any personal data that could identify participants removed before undertaking any analysis. The short-answer quiz was delivered first as the researcher assumed that, if multiple-choice quiz was conducted first, that might cause students to transfer some answers from the multiple-choice to the short-answer quiz, and that this would skew the results. Results from the quizzes required no data treatment or filtering (Brown, 2011), with results stored by the Google Forms 'Responses' function in Google Sheets. This data was also processed by Google Forms visualization tools with descriptive results presented, and allowing for descriptive analyses to occur.

Short-answer

The first conducted quiz was based on the vocabulary book by Nation (2018), *4000 Essential Words 1*, and included only short-answer questions that were created to assess the English vocabulary knowledge of intermediate level learners. As assumed by O'Leary & Israel (2017, p. 1), "there are two major question types used in a questionnaire: open-ended — a blank answer space provided for a description or explanation, a list of items, numbers, or dates; and closed-ended — response choices provided (scale, ordered, unordered, or partial)." Therefore, short-answer questions refer to open-ended question types, and this type of question was used at an initial stage of research in order to obtain clear results. i.e., short-answer questions do not provide the hints to students that multiple-choice questions can contain.

A [...] is the knowledge and ability that allows you to do something well?
Ex: A snowboarder must have the right [...]s to do well.

Short answer text
....

Figure 1. An example of a short-answer question*

---

* *Note:* the original image is in color, reproduced here in gray scale, and used under creative commons license (2019).

However, to alleviate question difficulties, color images were associated with each of the example sentences in which the vocabulary being tested could be used, as in Figure 1. Every correct answer was graded with five points. The maximum possible grade for the quiz sums up to 75 points.

The Docs Editors Help (2019) page for Google Forms describes the types of rules for creating short-answer type quizzes using the platform. It demonstrates that a short-answer can be up to 500 characters or must contain a specific word. Therefore, we can classify Google Forms short-answer as an open-ended question format. Roth (1996) notes that open-ended questions demand higher-order thinking from students and may not leave a place for guessing with Hargreaves (1984) adding that this type of questions is more involving and spurs judgment and reasoning, whereas checkboxes, dropdown and multiple-choice questions are defined by O'Leary & Israel (2017) as closed-ended, with participants also limited by the alternatives presented for each stem (Foddy, 1993).

Multiple-choice
The stems for this quiz are based on questions similar to those of Nation (2018) and rely on the multiple-choice question type where: "Multiple-choice or objective response is a form of an objective assessment in which respondents are asked to select only correct answers from the choices offered as a list" (Carneson, Delpierre, & Masters, 2016, p. 3). The second quiz also assessed knowledge of English vocabulary, but the pictures were excluded. See Figure 2 for an example of the questions included in this quiz. The exclusion of images should make the format of multiple-choice more difficult, making it closer to the perceived difficulty of the short-answer quiz type. The point scale of this quiz is the same as in the short-answer quiz.

A [...] is the knowledge and ability that allows you to do something well?
Ex: A snowboarder must have the right [...]s to do well.
o   skill
o   habit
o   ability

Figure 2. Multiple-choice question-type example

Limitations of the study

The number of students who took the survey is twenty, and this limitation can be explained by organizational difficulties in conducting the study across two countries. The research was also conducted in a limited time frame, with only thirty teachers participating. Further limitations pertain to one educator having no teaching experience (being pre-service), and relying upon a sample of convenience.

Results and discussion

The findings and discussion fall into two sections. Teacher Survey discusses the Google Forms assortment of question types and includes information about teachers' preferences. Student Quizzes discusses students' output results that were revealed during the research.

Teacher survey

The teacher survey aims to determine preferences for choice of a cloud-based formative assessment platform (see Table 4), satisfaction rates with these platforms (see Table 5), and the question type that these teachers typically use with such platforms (see Table 6).

Choice of cloud-based formative assessment platform

The preferences of teachers concerning cloud-based platform use when conducting formative assessment are distributed across seven tools (see Table 4). *Google Forms* at 40% (*n*=12) was the most preferred platform followed by *Microsoft Forms* at 23.3% (n=7) and *Microsoft Word* at 16.7% (n=5). Teacher's choices for other platforms were divided across four cloud-based tools, namely: *Typeform* (10%, n=3), *Kahoot!* (6.7%, n=2), *QuestionPro* (3.3%, n=1), and *Quizlet* (3.3%, n=1).

Table 4. *Teacher choice of cloud-based formative assessment platform*

Platform Name	Portion	
	n	%
Google Forms	12	40
Kahoot!	2	6.7
Microsoft Forms	7	23.3
Microsoft Word	5	16.7
QuestionPro	1	3.3
Quizlet	1	3.3
Typeform	3	10
TOTAL RESPONSES	31	103.3

Note: Total percentage is higher due to multiple selection possibilities of participants

Satisfaction rates with cloud-based formative assessment platforms

Results of the teacher survey show that the satisfaction rates with the use of Google Forms is quite high with 12.5% (*n*=2) of the 16 teachers using this platform being very satisfied, 37.5% (*n*=6) satisfied, and 50% (*n*=8) showing a neutral attitude, as shown in Table 5. This indicates that for these participants there is a high rate of satisfaction with the Google Forms platform as a tool for formative assessment.

Table 5. *Breakdown of teacher satisfaction rates for those relying on the Google Forms platform*

Satisfaction Rate	Portion	
	n	%
Very satisfied	2	12.5
Satisfied	6	37.5
Neutral	8	50
Unsatisfied	0	0
Very unsatisfied	0	0
TOTAL RESPONSES	16	100

Question-type preference for use with cloud-based formative assessment platforms

As can be seen from the Table 6, the teachers' preferences for question types used with formative assessment are mostly distributed between multiple-choice 73.3% ($n=22$) and short-answer 70% ($n=21$) questions. Other questions were rated as paragraph 33.3% ($n=10$), checkboxes 13.3% ($n=4$), and dropdown 3.3% ($n=1$).

Table 6. *Teacher preferences of question types for formative assessment*

Platform Name	Portion	
	n	%
Checkboxes	4	13.3
Checkbox grid	0	0
Dropdown	1	3.3
Linear scale	0	0
Multiple-choice	22	73.3
Multiple-choice grid	0	0
Paragraph	10	33.3
Short-answer	21	70
TOTAL RESPONSES	58	193.2

Note: Total percentage is higher due to multiple selection possibilities of participants

The data obtained above was then used as a foundation for conducting student quizzes to answer research question number two, and sees both the multiple-choice type and the short-answer type questions used to develop two different quizzes for delivery utilizing the Google Forms platform.

Student quizzes

In this analysis, we will rely upon median distribution as it was described in the Methods section. For the multiple-choice quiz results the median value of the correct answers is 70, which is quite a high grade. In contrast, the short-answer quiz results show a median value of 50 points. This data answers research question two by illustrating that participants were able to obtain greater accuracy rates when undertaking formative assessment using a multiple-choice question-type on a cloud platform for delivery of quizzes (see Table 7).

Table 7. *Analysis of the Quizzes Response rates and Results*

	Short-Answer Quiz	Multiple-Choice Quiz
Number of Questions	15	15
Total Responses	20	20
	Total Points Distribution (x/75)	
Median	50	70

Note: the median value of 70 in the multiple-choice test is not skewed by the zero points obtained by one of the participants, while the average value of 67.14 is affected by the outlier in the short-answer quiz results.

The difference observed in table 7 may be attributed to the fact that open-ended questions force learners to be more focused, to use high order thinking skills, to be correct in spelling, and that they are also prone to typos (Züll, 2016). However, open-ended questions can be used to collect necessary information and to encourage participants (Züll, 2016). This is supported by the data, as 18 out of 20 students rightly responded 'habit' to one of the quiz questions. However, 5 of the 18 (27.8%) misspelled their answer, spelling 'habit' as 'habbit', seeing their answer marked as incorrect when completing the question:

    A [...] is a thing that you do often?
    Ex: smoking is a bad [...] that can kill you seeing.

The research also revealed that the characteristics of open-ended and close-ended questions are different in terms of the role that respondents take when answering them, with participants limited by the alternatives presented to them in close-ended questions, while in open-ended questions, they were able to express themselves more spontaneously (Foddy, 1993). In this case, the short-answer quiz, also revealed accuracy issues when students do so, and can be useful in terms of gathering more specific information about learners' skills, which a teacher could then use to help diagnose student problems and identifying the words students might have trouble spelling. Ultimately though, it was found that students performed better, in terms of accuracy, when presented with multiple-choice question types, and this is perhaps because they are familiar with this question-type the most and the limited set range of choices helps them settle on the correct response.

Conclusion

The unique aim of this chapter is that it sought to serve as a preliminary study investigating the preference of instructors when using cloud-based platforms for formative assessment, and how the most used question-types compare in terms of student accuracy rates when formative assessment is conducted using those platforms. It was found that teacher preferences for the delivery of formative assessment favored Google Forms, so this cloud-based platform was utilized for this research. Teacher preferences regarding question-type use when conducting formative assessment when using cloud-based platforms, such as Google Forms, was then determined to be that of either multiple-choice or short-answer type. Further, for students undertaking formative assessment with these question-types, multiple-choice sees them achieve higher answer accuracy rates but the short-answer quiz type can provide additional data for the teacher to use for diagnostic purposes. This findings are supported by other researchers (Roth, 1996; Ozuru, Briner, Kurby & McNamara, 2013). Further, Roth (1996) found that with open-ended questions students have to think harder and have less chances for guessing, with Ozuru, et al. (2013) claiming that "participants' levels of topic specific knowledge were found to be more strongly correlated with performance on multiple-choice questions than with performance on open-ended questions" (p. 224).

Overall, in terms of data analysis and quiz development, Google Forms was found to be a valuable tool for conducting the research for this chapter. It provides a large assortment of question types, ready-to-use templates, features for embedding videos and pictures, and statistical modules for simple analyses of responses which are available immediately after the quiz is taken, and requires no special skills on the part of educators who rely on use of the platform.

References

Brown, A. (2011). Measures of shape: Skewness and kurtosis. MATH200. Retrieved from http://web.ipac.caltech.edu

Carneson, J., Delpierre, G., & Masters, K. (2016). *Designing and Managing Multiple Choice Questions* (2nd ed). http://dx.doi.org/10.13140/RG.2.2.22028.31369

Castro, S. (2018). Google Forms Quizzes and Substition, Augmentation, Modification, and Redefinition (SAMR) Model Integration. *Issues and Trends in Educational Technology, 6*(2), 4-14.

Clay, B. (2001). *Is This a Trick Question? A Short Guide to Writing Effective Test Questions.* Kansas, USA: Kansas Curriculum Center, Kansas State Department of Education.

Creative Commons License. (2019). Image of snow boarder. Retrieved from https://commons.wikimedia.org/wiki/File:272-foto-de-snowboard.jpg?fbclid=IwAR3Cgljv QKJgnnfcK-hnNA0tNHA_acczvCSmTgzy_aOACr0ro-cPlP9P1C0

Docs Editors Help (2019). Set rules for your form. Help Center. Retrieved from https://support.google.com/docs/answer/3378864?fbclid=IwAR07e4rrsfibFG5yegd5u26cLFsaIWzM9Cjw7eDd4HErARbhzv3-curs8SI#short_answer

Fischer, G., & Konomi, S. (2005). *Innovative media in support of distributed intelligence and lifelong learning.* Proceedings of the Third IEEE International Workshop on Wireless and Mobile Technologies in Education. Los Alamitos, CA: IEEE Computer Society, WMTE, 3-10.

Foddy, W. (1993). *Constructing questions for interviews and questionnaires: Theory and practice in social research.* Cambridge: Cambridge University Press.

Fraenkel, J., Wallen, N., & Hyun, H. (2012). *How to design and evaluate research in education,* (8th ed.). USA: McGraw-Hill.

Godino, J., & Batanero, C. (2002). *Studying the median: A framework to analyze instructional processes in statistics education.* In B. Phillips (Ed.), ICOTS-6 Papers for School Teachers: International Association for Statistics Education.

Hallur, R. (2016). *Google Forms that made teacher's life easier: An experience and experimentation.* Special Issue of National Conference NCIEME 2016. Organized by Rajarambapu Institute of Technology and Walchand College, Sangli, India.

Hargreaves, D. (1984). Teachers' questions: Open, closed and half-open. *Educational Research, 26,* 46-51.

Kerlinger, D., & Fred, N. (*1973). Foundations of behavioral research* (2nd ed.). New York: Holt, Rinehart and Winston.

Lisa, M. (2008). *The SAGE encyclopedia of qualitative research methods.* Los Angeles: SAGE Publications.

Nation, P. (2018). *4000 essential English words, Book 1* (2nd ed.). USA: Compass Publishing.

Napitupulu, D., Rahim, R., Abdullah, D., Setiawan, M., Abdillah, L., Ahmar, A., & Simarmata, J. (2018). Analysis of student satisfaction toward quality of service facility. *Journal of Physics Conference Series, 954*(1).

O'Leary, J., & Israel G. (2017). The savvy survey #6c: Constructing closed-ended items for a questionnaire. IFAS Extension, University of Florida. Retrieved from http://edis.ifas.ufl.edu/pdffiles/pd/pd06800.pdf

Ozuru, Y., Briner, S., Kurby, C., & McNamara, D. (2013). Comparing comprehension measured by multiple-choice and open-ended questions. *Canadian Journal of Experimental Pyschology/Revue Canadienne de psychologie experimentale, 67*(3), 215-227, https://dx.doi.org/10/1037/a0032918

Roth, M. (1996). Teacher questioning in an open-inquiry learning environment: Interactions of context, content, and student responses. *Journal of Research in Science Teaching, 33, 710-735.*

Rousseeuw, P. (1991). Tutorial to robust statistics. *Journal of Chemometrics, 5*(1), 1-20.

Scrivener, J. (2011). *Learning teaching: The essential guide to English Language teaching* (3rd ed.). USA: MacMillan.

Vosylis, R., Žukauskienė, R., Romeris, M., & Malinauskienė, O. (2012). Comparison of internet based versus paper-and-pencil administered assessment of positive development indicators in adolescent's sample. *Pyschology, 45, 7-21.*

Watt S., Simpson C., McKillop, C., & Nunn V. (2002). Electronic course surveys: Does automating feedback and reporting give better results? *Assessment & Evaluation in Higher Education, 27*(4), 325-337.

Wright, D., Aquilino, W., & Supple, A. (1998). A comparison of computer-assisted and paper-and-pencil self-administered questionnaires in a survey on smoking, alcohol, and drug use. *Public Opinion Quarterly, 62*, 331–353.

Yun, G., & Trumbo, C. (2000). Comparative response to a survey executed by post, e-mail, & web form. *Journal of Computer-Mediated Communication., 6*(1).

Züll, C. (2016). Open-ended questions. *GESIS survey guidelines.* Mannheim, Germany: GESIS – Leibniz Institute for the Social Sciences, https://dx.doi.org/10.15465/gesis-sg_en_002

8. Exploring the Purdue Online Writing Lab (OWL) and a Flipped Approach: An Integration which Complements Language Learning

Ariadne Patricia Borges
TESOL-MALL Graduate Program, Woosong University

Abstract

The online availability of broad range technology-enhanced tools for teaching and learning has resulted in the development and restructuring of second language pedagogy, particularly in regards to improving learner output. Nunan (in Fareed, Ashraf & Bilal, 2016) argues that "writing is an extremely difficult cognitive activity which requires the learner to have control over various factors. These factors vary from academic background and personal interest of the writer to various psychological, linguistic and cognitive phenomena" (p. 82). Three challenges that teachers and learners face in second language writing include: emerging new written genres and their consequences for the notion of prescriptive writing; the reproduction and/or modification of 'descriptive and prescriptive writing' examples as means of learning, which can lead to the possibility of plagiarism; and how learners can learn to develop their own voice, and their second-language identity needs when practicing their writing skills (Walker & White, 2017). With these challenges in mind, this paper has been inspired by two elements: the exploration of the Online Writing Lab (OWL) at Purdue University; and seeking to integrate use of this site with a flipped classroom model that aims to present an overview for acquiring and enhancing learners' writing skills, strategies, motivation, engagement, and making meaning from experience. Therefore, this paper will not only educate language teachers in the use of the online resource, The Purdue Online Writing Lab (2019), but it will also provide a foundation for what it means to adapt teaching and learning approaches to a flipped classroom model and to the technology-enhanced learning and teaching approaches that have arisen as a result of the fourth industrial revolution.

The Purdue Online Writing Lab (OWL) and a Flipped Classroom Approach

The Purdue Online Writing Lab (2019) is a resourceful website that continuously promotes support for the student population of Purdue University in West Lafayette in Indiana, local literacy initiatives, and the global body of professional ESL/EFL community who are looking for assistance in their development as writers. Therefore, writers and educators in need of assistance, particularly in regards to writing style, and citation assistance, can benefit from the materials they provide. The Paiz (2017) research article on general OWL survey findings presented the penetration of general OWL use in the L2 writing classroom, with data collected by the survey showing that 79.7% of 133 respondents use OWLs in some capacity when teaching L2 writing. This in turn reveals that these online resources are indeed useful for those teachers when they conduct writing initiatives with learners. The flipped classroom approach is a pedagogical model in which traditional lectures and homework completion is applied in reverse, and a technique which also allows learners to collaborate with interactive online content to expand their learning progress. It is usually divided into two learning environments: outside and inside the classroom, with both sides needing to be integrated for this model to be effective (Basal, 2015). Such a lesson delivery framework is commonly applied alongside three learning elements: the first is a pre-class element (flexible environment) in which students choose when and where they will learn, the second is a during-class performance (active involvement in knowledge construction and learning strategies), and the third is a post-class element (practice, performance, and feedback).

Using the Online Writing Lab and a Flipped Classroom Approach

The Purdue Online Writing Lab (2019; hereafter *OWL*) can be used as reference material both inside and outside the classroom setting, and its collection of online resources offer a wide variety of writing materials that address a variety of topics such as the general writing process, teacher and tutor resources, subject-specific resources, and online writing exercises. For example, for adult educators, the resources on academic writing can be adapted for the purposes of in-class instruction on general writing processes such as academic writing, common writing assignments, grammar, visual rhetoric, mechanics, and punctuation to name a few.

Second, the teacher and tutor section of the *OWL* contains teacher resources and Microsoft PowerPoint presentations, for example, those on how to write workshops for graduate students, different types of lesson plans for teaching writing, and activities on writing in terms of how to avoid plagiarism. In addition, the *OWL Purdue YouTube channel* (OWL Purdue, 2019) offers a series of vidcasts which can be introduced during table talk or as a warm-up part of a lesson on the basics of grammar, visual rhetoric, and the ins and outs of essay formatting on the application of APA (American Psychological Association) and MLA (Modern Language Association) styles. Another form of applying their online resources is the use of subject-specific resources on different subjects (e.g., writing in literature; writing terms and theory; writing for poetry and film, writing in the social sciences, healthcare, journalism, art history; and, job search writing).

Finally, it can be integrated into a flipped classroom approach. Further, resources and materials applicable to in-class and out-of-classroom learning can be found under the *OWL*, and these include exercises which provide language practice in paraphrasing, sentence structure, style, grammar, and other aspects. This allows the site to be integrated into a flipped classroom approach, and one where students can study materials at their own pace, and this will be influenced by both the use of educational technology outside of class and active learning during class time (Han, 2015). Using the *OWL* is of particular value to students interested in both the writing process and in accessing resources which address writing steps, and those that provide guidance, revision, as well as materials including printable sheets and Microsoft PowerPoint presentations with advice.

Types of Benefits that Exist for Educators and Learners

E-learning is an invaluable resource which focuses on students' individual learning needs, and since the *OWL* houses writing resources and instructional material to support students and teachers, there is a variety of conventional benefits which educators and learners can utilize to meet their goals and maximize their learning outcomes, while also allowing for both to post their writings on the internet. Here are some examples of the benefits that teachers and learners can find when using this online resource: learn-at-own pace, practicality, access to training, and application of theory.

In regards to learn-at-own pace, the *OWL* can be used in a way that provides a means for teachers and students to work together to meet their goals and outcomes while also being able to meet the individual students' learning curve and style.

Practicality, meaning workload reduction, may see use of the *OWL* afford instructors a benefit by allowing them to quickly develop assessment materials, and OWL provides online grammar exercises which instructors can utilize in class for assessment (e.g., adjective versus adverbs, articles, tense consistency, and sentence structure). All of the above in turn can be employed within lessons plans as quick assessments, which target student's experience levels by focusing on their linguistic accuracy (The Purdue Online Writing Lab, 2019a).

Furthermore, the *OWL* can deliver learners and instructors with training opportunities that may provide them with a means of improving upon their writing knowledge and skills, along with tasks and activities that can be integrated within lesson plans. For example, one way both teachers and students can further enhance their writing skills are through the section on world Englishes which exemplify classroom applications and activities, these *OWL* classroom applications and activities provide theoretical frameworks, which can be augmented during classroom instruction. For example, writing prompts which help teachers pluralize students' perceptions through classroom activities, discussions, and writing assignments (The Purdue Online Writing Lab, 2019b). Important here is understanding that the application of pedagogical theory to the activities and delivery of learning content which can achieved through a flipped approach, in which, learning choices are presented to students (Basal, 2015), and at the same time enabling teachers to embrace authentic content not only through online texts but also through multimedia, vidcasts, and Microsoft PowerPoint presentations of which the *OWL* contains. For these technologies to be used successfully relies on the pedagogy behind the technology (Kent, 2019) as well as the humanware, and not the hardware or software being employed (Basal, 2015).

The Elements behind an Effective Flipped Classroom Model

There are several elements behind an effective flipped classroom approach which teachers and learners can take into consideration. To begin with, teachers will need to explain how and why this approach is beneficial to their classroom pedagogy (Basal, 2015). Laying out the elements provides a much-needed understanding for students to comply with such an approach. The elements are:

shifting of workload, pedagogy (conceptual framework, and the collecting of student resources and understanding), pre-class cognitive engagement, learning space and time (leading to metacognitive development of students), adding value to learning, and the interactive engagement of students. These elements in turn are the foundation of a model which facilitates the learning process and one that relies upon the incorporation of internet-based technologies both inside and outside of the classroom (Basal, 2015). Therefore, a flipped classroom model can be described as a collaboration of pedagogical approaches which aim to connect aspects of socialization with technological enhancement, in terms of e-learning, to effectively promote learning and instruction (Guy & Marquis, 2016).

Shifting workload
To initially employ the use of a flipped classroom approach, teachers will need to decrease scheduled class time and homework to allow students to recognize and understand that their workload has shifted and not increased. Here are some examples that teachers might consider when shifting the workload.

First, teachers can hold meetings with their students to discuss the running of the classroom and what it will entail, with this perhaps fostering a positive school culture where the students take on increased responsibility for the classroom and develop a sense of ownership of their learning space whether this takes place at home or at school. Hence the location of the learning space does not matter and in time, students may increasingly gain respect and value their education. Just as important is making sure to delegate the workload and the sharing of tasks with students and colleagues if you are working in a co-teaching context (Schindler, 2016).

Pedagogy

In a flipped classroom model teachers need to consider making their pedagogy as simple as possible, by taking into consideration the four pillars of F-L-I-P, and focusing on intentional content and, therefore, teaching only what needs to be taught to enable students to meet learning outcomes and to maintain their focus on learning and developing their education (FLN, 2014). Further, there is no need to come up with all lesson ideas in advance. Bergmann and Sams (in Sung, 2015) argue that in turn instruction time can be applied through the use of lectures previously recorded until content becomes outdated, which allows instructors to spend more time helping students comprehend the lesson instead of developing lesson ideas in advance during a busy school season. For example, there is a distinction between writing lessons and planning learning – teaching in a flipped classroom model is about focusing on continually evaluating, adapting, and improving learning outcomes. Professional educators who apply a flipped model continually observe their learners, provide them feedback, and assess outcomes, while also determining content that needs to be taught, and what materials learners can explore on their own, and maintaining flexible expectations of learner outcomes (FLN, 2016). To this end, a conceptual framework is required, and one that allows learning to take place in a scaffolded manner, such as activities created being accessible to all students through differentiation and feedback, and as a result students become actively involved in the learning process as they participate and evaluate their own learning development (FLN, 2016). Therefore, explaining this element to learners may help clarify the intention of implementing particular materials and resources into the lesson design. There are various sources which teachers can use to develop a learning framework. For example, Bloom's revised digital taxonomy (Kent, 2015), the technology integration matrix (TIM, 2018), and the substitution, augmentation, modification, redefinition (SAMR) model (Puentedura, 2006). In addition, tracking progress utilizing a technological approach (for example, using a learning management system), would allow grading to be completed faster. In this case, applications such as Grade Me for Moodle, and Unicheck are two examples that an instructor can utilize to provide timely feedback to learners via notes or comments on their assignments and grades. Also, the use of a learning management system (LMS) will help with presenting all tasks/activities in an organized fashion connecting the outside and inside aspects of the learning process (Basal, 2015).

Pre-class Cognitive Engagement
This aspect focuses upon the idea of having learners experience the value of pre-class cognitive acquaintance with created intentional content (lessons, units) that are accessible and relevant to their learning language and culture through the engagement and interactivity of various approaches and activities. This might include using Plickers which is a QR-based formative assessment tool that takes the technology out of the students' hands (Kent, 2019). In a study conducted to gain insight into student persepectives on different study platforms, Mendez (2019) found that students who experienced Plickers liked the use of this assessment tool, particularly for its ease of use, being able to receive anonymous peer instruction while using it, and that it worked with small sized classes. Also instructors can use Actions on Google where templates can be used to create voice-activated learning for students using vocabulary flashcards. Either of these tools in a warm-up allows students to engage in target language practice individually, with short one-on-one quizzes, and when used in a group activity context would allow them to engage in discussions with their peers. The introduction of the OWL can then be utilized as the foundation for developing creative in- and out-of-classroom content (e.g., student's assessment of citation styles, which can then be assessed in fun, informative and

interactive ways). In this regard the OWL can assist students and teachers practice, learn, and gather data of and for student understanding.

Learning Space and Time
In terms of space and time, when taking into consideration a flipped classroom approach, it is important to evaluate the space in which the students will engage with e-learning and the allocated time available. That is to say, when designing a flipped model lesson by carefully considering a flexible environment, instructors will need to establish both space and time frames which allow learners to interact and reflect upon their learning as need (FLN, 2016). This in turn serves the elements of metacognitive development of students, and provides added value in which the teacher provides students with a cognitive model for learners to follow, and one that progresses from lower to higher levels of thinking, which would also allow students to reflect upon and become aware of their own learning development (Bloom's Taxonomy: Teacher Planning Kit, n.d.).

Adding Value
Lesson formatting and design should be perceived by educational institutions and their instructors as providing added value to student learning, with those instructors guiding students with content and materials that move learners beyond the knowledge/comprehension stage to where they can start to utilize higher-order thinking skills that can in turn trigger the application, analysis, synthesis, and evaluation of knowledge (Bloom's Taxonomy: Teacher Planning Kit, n.d.). By designing cognitive objectives for a lesson plan, educators can increase students' knowledge and understanding of materials, and one way this can be accomplished is by looking at key verbs for each level of Bloom's revised 2001 Hierarchy (Bixler, 2018). For example, remember – using memory to recall facts and definitions

(recognize), understand – constructing meaning from knowledge (understand), apply – using procedures to deliver task/activity (demonstrate), analyze– breaking materials into parts to determine relationships (analyze), evaluate – critiquing materials based on checking against given criteria, and create – gathering materials to create a product (construct/design).

Interactivity and cognitive engagement
Also, the provision of interactivity and cognitive engagement with learning can also be considered by [m]any educator(s) as an indispensable structure to be added to a flipped classroom model. Such content could perhaps be made in a way that provides learners with social interaction both in the classroom and vie e-learning and in ways that might prove cognitively engaging (e.g., by providing group discussion-based activities, reflections, active listening, and proactive work). In terms of OWL use, this could be achieved by assisting learners in taking on a new perspective as writers with teachers and learners following a three-step model that sees them:

- embracing the 'write' attitude, believing in the development of a healthy writing habit and valuing improvement and stress-free productivity;
- managing and controlling the factors that facilitate the ability to write; and,
- engaging in practice – deliberate practice which is focused and persistent for the purpose of improving performance (Goodson, 2013).

Lending the OWL to TESOL
The *OWL* can be adapted and/or made suitable for the teaching of English as a second or a foreign language in numerous forms. First, teachers need to consider how learning online can become adapted both in and out of their traditional classroom settings, and there are quite a variety of ways to do this. For example,

consider the idea of whole or small group activities in which the teacher may adapt material developed by the OWL, such as teaching the basics of MLA formatting (choosing a font, spacing, and margins, and creating headers and a title). Also, making use of the available vidcasts is possible, and these may be shown on an interactive whiteboard, or teachers can have their students watch them on various writing resources on their own screens outside of the classroom, and have groups of students present what they have learned when returning to the class and then lead a discussion on the topic. Another suggestion would be to apply a flipped-classroom model in which students are assigned tasks to complete outside of class, which would involve online homework with worksheets on particular writing themes (e.g., tips on college level writing; plagiarism and EFL/ESL writers; writing for a specific audience). Following on from this, and in class, learners would then engage with hands-on and interactive activities. In such a model, teachers may also need to consider those students who have mastered content, and these students would then need to be provided with a challenge and a means of solidifying their learning. This could be achieved by allowing these students to take on more self-directed learning, and to also have them tutor those students who have not yet mastered the concepts being taught. Not only will this help to develop further higher thinking skills in both kinds of student, but it will also promote responsibility and learner autonomy as Kvashnina and Martynko (2016) illustrate, this development can take into consideration Bloom's revised taxonomy for developing students' thinking skills and knowledge, in which "students are first organized to deal online with the lower levels of cognitive work" allowing them to not only recall previously learned knowledge but also that recently acquired, promoting student responsibility and independence in regards to learning, prior to developing a "focus on the higher forms of cognitive work including application, analysis, synthesis, evaluation, and creation" (1).

Guidelines for Using the OWL Online Writing Lab for Research

In terms of research for teachers and learners, the *OWL* provides guidelines for users, by presenting a series of three points:
- focusing writers on the kind of information that they will be looking for (e.g., facts, opinions, research studies, and analyses);
- redirecting writers to where they can find the information that they are looking for (e.g., scholarly interpretations of literature in academic periodicals and books, or searching for local history in the city archives and at a library); and,
- guiding the writer at narrowing down a search by examining the amount of information that they will need.

Online Resource Evaluation: Implementation and Integration levels

As might be expected, there are a few ways which educators can evaluate resources and their own use of technology.

Implementation

Teachers will find that developing a step-by-step evaluation of the online resources that they seek to employ will further guide them to accurately prescribe the knowledge and materials available through such resources, and the accuracy of their application for meeting desired outcomes or goals, as Fotos and Browne (2004) argue educators who have students study on the internet should take into account an evaluation of the sites learners access in the same manner as they would any other teaching material. To begin with, technology integration analysis and evaluation can be conducted in order to generate conceptual models regarding the implementation and use of a resource; or templates, and rubrics to help educators evaluate the technology or online resources that they wish to use by considering how its content best fits students and teachers, reflecting on how the resource fits pedagogically, how it suits in terms of classroom usability, considering the resources it provides, and the ways in which it will be assessed (Kent, 2019).

Integration Levels
Educators may find the technology integration matrix (TIM, 2018) useful to determine their level of technology integration, by looking at the section on professional learning. Some examples teachers may wish to follow in order to help determine their level of technology understanding are watching videos, exploring the meaning of a specific level within one of the TIM's columns, and gaining understanding of those characteristics. In addition, instructors can review previous lessons they have taught and from that perspective then consider how they might then improve upon the use of technology for teaching. Further, in terms of being able to investigate learners' needs, the gathering of valuable student-population input can be analyzed into three subcategories: necessities, lacks, and wants. Creating a checklist of demographics (educational, motivational, and aspirational variables) can also help with instructional planning for the L2 (second language) writing class or course in terms of meeting the aforementioned learner needs (Ferris & Hedgcock, 2014).

Tools/Resources Available for the Creation of a Flipped Classroom Approach

Since technology has been the catalyst for movements in the development of flipped classroom approaches, there are numerous technological tools with which teachers and students can utilize to engage with learning content. For the purposes of this paper, the tools and resources available on the *OWL* will be primarily discussed, followed by a brief listing of those that can be applied to the development of a flipped classroom approach.

OWL Resources
The *OWL* provides an extensive list of online resources to help guide writers in the development of writing skills and strategies. These resources are offered in the following formats: online informational texts, online information text activities, Microsoft PowerPoints, and vidcasts hosted on the *OWL Purdue YouTube channel* (OWL Purdue, 2019). The content includes:
- General writing, which covers the basics of the writing process, which then moves toward more challenging writing such as that involved with academic writing at the graduate school level (e.g., writing a research statement; research and citations, which covers topics such as applying research, along with correct use of current APA, MLA, and Chicago citation styles).
- Resources available in Microsoft PowerPoint format and PDF. Including those on teaching writing, preventing plagiarism, translingual writing, and email etiquette (e.g., how to write when contacting a professor).
- Other resources that focus upon subject-specific writing, job-search writing, writing for those with English as a second language, and *OWL* vidcasts which cover a variety of topics on writing, rhetoric, grammar, and the basic formatting rules of various citation styles.

Other Tools
There are a variety of other tools that teachers can use to create a flipped classroom approach for their learners. These might include tools for:
- screencasting, such as *Screencastify* (Google Chrome extension), *Screencast-o-Matic* (PC and Mac), and *Snagit* (PC and Mac); and those for

- creating videos, *Classflow* (used to make interactive class presentations), *EdPuzzle* (develop interactive videos using a question-based format), and *TES Teach* (to create lessons, projects, presentation, quizzes, and discussions).

Considerations for Crafting a Lesson: Potential for Implementing the Owl Purdue with a Flipped Classroom Approach

It is important to understand that the student population today is vastly different from other times in terms of how they engage in learning and the tools/resources applicable to them (Kent, 2019). Therefore, self-directed learning is considered to be beneficial and when applying a flipped model it could be an alternative approach to adopt when aiming for self-directed learning. As Hayati (2001) discusses, self-directed students show awareness of responsibility towards their learning process because not only will they monitor their work, but they will also view problems as challenges, and are willing to try new things. Therefore, self-directed learning can promote motivation, persistence, learning autonomy, self-confidence and self-discipline (Hayati, 2001) allowing learners to become more effective in a flipped model classroom. So the question is, how could teachers develop a lesson implementing the *OWL* a flipped classroom model? To answer this, there are five steps to consider.

1. Decide how the technology, resources, and tools that you will use complement the lesson aims and objectives. Remember that the main purpose behind any digital language learning opportunity presented to students is to enhance the learning and teaching process by the affordances arising from use of the technology (Kent, 2019). The *OWL* offers extensive online informational texts and vidcasts which can be adapted for classroom use and homework.

2. Decide which vidcast or online resources you and your students can use to practice writing and to develop their language skills. Also, selecting topics that students struggle with and have them prepare questions and answers to help explain the concept during class time allows collaboration with their peers, sharing of meanings, and perhaps leading to present the topic and discuss it with the class.
3. Explain the pros of such approach, making sure to establish rules and accountability before distributing or assigning tasks/activities. Equally as important is teaching your students how to watch, take notes, and engage proactively with the content (e.g., watching a whole vidcast on APA basics and not taking notes, then watching it again, taking notes, and adding information or questions.)
4. Fourth, access for all means making sure that all learners have the technology needed to practice in their homes or during any time or space desired. If not, creating a contingency plan with alternative methods of access will need to be arranged.
5. Leave the easy content for outside the classroom setting. If students have viewed certain content on vidcast, from Microsoft PowerPoint, or read it on an informational text online, there is no need to waste classroom time on rewatching the same content unless it is integrated into review.

Summary

Exploring the use of the *OWL* and a flipped-classroom model led to providing answers to the following questions:
- What is the online writing lab and a flipped model, and how could it be used?
- What types of benefits exist for using an OWL?

- What are the elements and effectiveness of using a flipped-classroom model?
- How can the OWL lend itself to TESOL?
- How can use of online resources be evaluated in terms of implementation and integration levels?
- What tools are available for the creation of a flipped classroom approach?
- What considerations are required to create a lesson using the OWL and a flipped classroom approach?

It is suggested that educators wanting to integrate use of the OWL and a flipped classroom approach into their teaching continue further evaluation, reflection, and research.

References

Basal, A. (2015). The implementation of a flipped classroom in foreign language teaching. *Turkish Online Journal of Distance Education, 16*(4), 28-37. https://doi.org/10.17718/tojde.72185

Bixler, B. (2018). Instructional goals and objectives. Retrieved from http://www.personal.psu.edu/bxb11/Objectives

Bloom's Taxonomy: Teacher Planning Kit. (n.d.) Retrieved from https://www.cebm.net/wp-content/uploads/2016/09/Blooms-Taxonomy-Teacher-Planning-Kit.pdf

Fareed, M., Ashraf, A., & Bilal, M. (2016). ESL learners' writing skills: Problems, factors and suggestions. *Journal of Education & Social Sciences, 4*(2), 82-93. https://doi.org/10.20547/jess0421604201

FLN. (2014). The Four Pillars of F-L-I-P™. Flipped Learning Network. Retrieved from http://flippedlearning.org/wp-content/uploads/2016/07/FLIP_handout_FNL_Web.pdf

Fotos, S., & Browne, C. (2004). *New perspectives on CALL for second language acquisition*. USA: Routledge.

Goodson, P. (2013). *Becoming an academic writer: 50 exercises for paced, productive, and powerful writing*. USA: Sage Publications, Inc.

Guy, R., & Marquis, G. (2016). The flipped classroom: A comparison of student performance using instructional videos and podcasts versus the lecture-based model of instruction. *Issues in Informing Science and Information Technology, 13*, 1-13.

Kent, D. (2015). Using iPedagogy with mobile devices to extend language learning strategies with Bloom's (revised) digital taxonomy. *TEC, 19*(1), 27-30.

Kent, D. (2019). Teaching in the time of digital language learning. The fourth industrial revolution and education: Digital language learning and teaching, June 01. Daejeon, Republic of Korea. Retrieved from https://www.youtube.com/watch?v=wxKOdSaqpHs&list=PLPpILLiV4jEND8SwXIA1qCNCif1tL4fhN&index=4

Han. Y. (2015). Successfully flipping the ESL classroom for learner autonomy. *NYS TESOL Journal, 2*(1), 98-109.

Hayati, A. (2001). *Self-directed learning, ERIC Digest*. Bloomington, IN: ERIC Clearing house on Reading English and Communication.

Kvashina, O., & Martynko, E. (2016). Analyzing the potential of flipped classroom in ESL teaching. *International Journal of Emerging Technologies in Learning, 11*(3), 71-73, https://doi.org/10.3991/ijet.v11i03.5309

Mendez, J. (2019). Instructor and student experiences with in-class polling options. ASEE IL-IN Section Conference 3. Retrieved from https://docs.lib.purdue.edu/aseeil-insectionconference/2019/assess/3

OWL Purdue. (2019). The Purdue Online Writing Lab YouTube Channel. Retrieved from https://www.youtube.com/user/OWLPurdue/featured

Paiz, J. (2017). Uses and attitudes towards OWLs as L2 writing support tools. *The Asian EFL Journal Quarterly, 19*(1), 56-80.

Puentedura, R. (2006). Transformation, technology, and education. Retrieved from http://hippasus.com/resources/tte

Schindler, E. (2016). *Learning how to delegate as a leader*. USA: O'Reilly Media, Inc.
Sung, K. (2015). A case study on a flipped classroom in an EFL content course. *Multimedia Assisted Language Learning, 18*(2), 159-187.
The Purdue Online Writing Lab. (2019a). OWL // Purdue Writing Lab (College of Liberal Arts). Retrieved from https://owl.purdue.edu
The Purdue Online Writing Lab. (2019b). Adjective or Adverb Exercise 1 // Purdue Writing Lab. Retrieved from https://owl.purdue.edu/owl_exercises/grammar_exercises/adjective_or_adverb/adjective_or_adverb_exercise_1.html
The Purdue Online Writing Lab. (2019c). Classroom Applications and Activities // Purdue Writing Lab. Retrieved from https://owl.purdue.edu/owl/english_as_a_second_language/world_englishes/classroom_applications_and_activities.html.
TIM. (2018). Technology Integration Matrix. A project of the Florida Center for Instructional Technology. Retrieved from https://fcit.usf.edu/matrix
Walker, A., & White, G. (2017). *Technology Enhanced Language Learning: Connecting theory and practice.* United Kingdom: Oxford University Press.

9. Will English Remain a Lingua Franca in the Industry 4.0 Era?

Wu Yang (Miranda Wu)
Hunan University of Technology and Business,
People's Republic of China
Endicott College of International Studies, Woosong University

Introduction – English Language Future in the Industry 4.0 Era[*]

The world is changing in many ways, and one of the key things that will have a huge impact on our future is artificial intelligence (AI) which is an area of computer science that emphasizes the creation of intelligent machines that work and react like humans. Some of the activity computers with artificial intelligence are designed to include are speech recognition, computer vision, deep learning involving processing knowledge, reasoning, problem solving, perception, planning and ability to manipulate and move objects like humans (robotics), neural machine translation (NMT), and so on. AI has brought us into the fourth industrial revolution in the 21st century, and if the previous industrial revolutions empowered human beings mechanically, the fourth industry revolution with AI is going to revolutionize our cognitive powers. Moreover, people are arguing that AI is going to replace both our manual and mental labor, and if so, what kind of influence is it going to have on the future of the English language, and on the ways of teaching and learning it?

English language has a unique power. Out of more than 7,000 languages in the world, with 50% of the world population speaking only 10 of them (BBC News, 2018), with English, Chinese, Spanish, Arabic, and Hindi-Urdu being the 5 behemoths (languages spoken by a large population), the English language in particular has held a position of unprecedented dominance for

Note: Part of the research findings in this chapter were published in Wu (2019).

global business and communication since the 20th century. A quarter of the world population speak at least some level of English because they are students in high schools and universities worldwide (Ibid). The unassailable importance of English can be seen in all social and economic spheres. However, the prominent performance of the People's Republic of China (hereafter China, or the PRC) is empowering Mandarin with increasing economic strength. Together with the disruptive impact of artificial intelligence (AI) powered technologies, i.e., machine translation technologies in the ongoing era of the fourth industrial revolution (Industry 4.0), the English language is experiencing transformation in varieties and application (Feng, 2018). Will English remain in a position of preeminence in the 21st century and maintain its hold as a global language?

In the past two centuries, communicating globally has been in English. English, having gained world dominance since Britain's rise in the 19th Century to be the world's hegemony state. This language behemoth has been reinforced with the United States of Americas' (USA) rise to be a world superpower both in the economic and political sectors throughout the course of the 20th Century. Ever since then, communicating globally has seen the emergence of the globalization of the English language (Zhang, 2016). It is now an important medium for science and technology, business trade, and for popular culture. For a time, people opted to believe that English would become increasingly popular with 78.8% (n=394) of a total of 500 participants involved in the research for this chapter believing that for the past and present, communicating globally has meant communicating in English: they are able to talk to more people even if they don't know them; they are able to travel confidently to many places in the world; working in an international organization requires English language proficiency as an important passport; and in some countries like India, English language is not only a language of communication, but also a language of class and status (BBC

News, 2018). In some societies, proficiency in English is also an indicator of intelligence and the ability to command its use is essential for social acceptance, among the 351 participants who replied whoa agree and strongly agree, 89% of them are from countries with English as second language. In the PRC, English is no longer taught to tiny elite groups; it is now taught to a wider range of the general population from preschool age, where parents want their children to gain exposure to English as early as possible in order to provide what they consider to be a better start in life, according to 80.6% ($n=403$) of the participants.

So is English going to squeeze out other less widely spoken languages? Is it going to be more uniform with the use of the internet? Or will it be pushed aside by another language?

With economic and political globalization, English has been in constant change in regards to its vocabulary and structure, and there are controversies in the perception of English language development (Finneran, 1987). The internet is increasing chances of English to display fragmentation and diversity and it is fractured into many other languages in the same way as Latin is divided into French, Italian, Spanish and Portuguese (Gong, 2000).

However, in the world of computers, robots, and prevailing online social media, will English remain the behemoth of all languages? In the context of computer technology, if computers or robots will one day be available to translate every language into every other language, why should everybody learn English if it is not their first language? Is English going to be squeezed out by another language? Does British English still have a global role? Is Mandarin and the rise of China posing a threat to the long-term dominance of English as world's lingua franca? The British linguist Graddol (1997) stated that by the middle of the 21st century, English will probably lose its dominance but remain as one of the world's oligopoly languages along with Arabic, Hindi-Urdu, and Mandarin. English might be the world's last lingua franca (a common language used by speakers of different languages), and the days of English as a world language may be countable (McArthur, 1996).

How would English change itself when the world tide of AI powered technologies washes over it? What are the influencing factors that will contribute to this change? How will AI-powered innovative digital technologies change the way that people use and learn the English language?

The future of the English language
It is truly interesting to verify what Graddol (1997) has predicted. He suggested that the end of 20th century will be followed by a global transition period which would last for about 20 years. The famous British Council English 2000 Project (British Council, 1995) concluded that, with 1400 million speakers and a growing demand by the remaining four fifths of the world's population, the status of English will be the unquestionably dominant language for global communication. However, the future of English is hard to predict according to Crystal (1997), holding a view that when a language has reached genuine world status, there is hence no precedents that may assist in seeing what might then happen to the language. The proposed 20 years of rapid change and global transition (Graddol, 1997) came to an end in 2017, and it was said to be a very critical time that would come to provide implications for the future of English based on the patterns of usages and the general public attitude toward the language. Krauss (1992) has argued that the future of English will not be in immediate danger but it is not wise to foresee a remarkable dominance after a world new world order has been established in the 21st century, especially when some regions and domains have pioneered in social, economic, demographic transformations. Crystal (1997) negated that the development of English as the world's largest second language would exclude other languages being spoken in the world. People learn English

as a second language but they do not give up their native language completely. The spread of English around the world has essentially then greatly increased the number of people who speak two or more languages, but Wan (2015) concludes that the preeminent position of the English language would be challenged by some other major languages with the increasing deeper and wider trend of globalization.

Influencing factors of language development

Gong (2000) points out that state power plays an important role in the macro-development of language, and predicted that English could be an international language in the early 21st century. Political and economical strength of a country affects how its mainstream language develops, and this can be seen from the fluctuation in the number of language speakers for the five main languages of Europe during the years 1868 to 1921 (Grimes, 1996). See table 1.

Table 1. *The number of speakers for the five main European languages from 1868 to 1921 in millions*

Population of Speakers in Millions for the Five main European Languages by Year					
Year	English	German	Spanish	French	Russian
1868	60	52	40	45	45
1890	111	75	42	51	75
1900	116	75	44	45	70
1912	150	90	52	47	106
1921	170	87.5	62	45	120.5

These five languages developed very differently in the European region with French notably stagnant, Spanish remaining stable in its number of speakers; speakers of German having rising to 90 million in 1912, but decreasing slightly to 87.5 million in 1921, English users soared by 283%, and Russian increased by 265%. What made the big difference? The German empire was founded in 1871, the government began to devote itself to the building of comprehensive national strength upon its original lose of control over the union, and by the end of the century Germany was at the forefront of European countries and the number of German language speakers had increased, but its defeat in the first world war accomplished a slight decrease among its speakers (Skudlik, 1992). In the second half of the 19th century, Russia grabbed large tracts of land in central and East Asia in its territorial expansion and brought large populations under its control, and the number of Russian speakers soared (Ibid). As for Britain, after overtaking France as the leading power in the western world during the first industrial revolution, through various means of colonialism, it finally came to the 60-year Victorian Era, where it would reign over a quarter of global territory and a quarter of the world's population (Viereck, 1996). The number of English speakers has been increasing markedly, especially with the United States of America achieving hegemony in the 20th century (Kachru, 1985).

The development of political and economic power and the rise of comprehensive national strength among the above-mentioned countries coincides with changes in the number of language speakers in the countries shown in table 1. The correlation between national strength and language development can also be seen historically (Leith, 1996).

Melitz (2008) stated that language is important in foreign trade. With the enrichment and development of human economic activities, especially the accelerated flow of production materials, goods, and the labor force promoted by globalization in the world, language has become an important element or even a key element in economic activities, whether it be at the individual level, organizational level or national level. Driven by the two driving forces of population flow and informatization, language contributes more and more to the economy, so that it becomes an economic phenomenon that cannot be ignored (Lohmann, 2011). Language development is closely related to the revolutions in science and technology in human history. Language vocabulary, semantics and word combinations in languages evolve in accordance with these revolutions (Webster, 1789). The mingle and immersion of different languages is seen to occur alongside science and technology revolutions. The impact continues to be more profound in the era of knowledge and big data economy in which human languages and technology are increasingly interlinked (Yuan, 2012). The impact of science and technology on language evolution is mainly reflected in the promotion of strong development and dissemination of some languages, such as English in the 20th Century. Meanwhile, it also accelerates the weakening and even extinction of some local languages (Zhong et al., 2010).

The shift in economic relations will likely have a profound, but as yet poorly understood, effect on the popularity and use of different languages. Languages have economic strength. It is obvious that a language which is spoken by wealthier countries is more attractive to learners than one which provides no access to personal betterment or lucrative markets. The language of an economically strong community is attractive to learn because of its business potential. Knowledge of the language potentially opens up the market for producers to penetrate a market if they know the language of the potential customer (Ammon 1995).

Coulmas (2012) suggests that a corroboration of the attractiveness of Japanese language with the rise in the number of students enrolling in courses worldwide in Japanese as a foreign language closely mirrored a rise in the value of the Japanese yen against the US dollar during the period 2002 to 2012. The trend of hybrid languages possibly poses a threat to the English language. The rise of China and Mandarin likely poses a challenge to the dominance of English with Mandarin potentially gaining popularity because of its increasing importance in international business trade. It is definitely advantageous to communicate with Chinese businessmen in Mandarin in order to purchase 'Made in China' products from the PRC or those that are made in Chinese factories located in other countries. Mandarin is also seen to be gaining popularity as there is an increasing number of people learning Mandarin from the PRC supported Confucius Institutes (Wu & Kam, 2018). Qian (2006) concludes that language would be a mountain that stands in the way for Chinese companies going global. He revealed that China could not compete in the global reallocation of human resources due to the fact that Mandarin has a long way to go to become a working language of economics and commerce. Yet, at a more fundamental level, there is a problem that does not seem to be getting enough attention. The reorganization of market resources under globalization requires not only the flow of products and capital, but also the flow of human resources. Chinese enterprises which aim to surf in the globalization tide need a large amount of international talent. This talent will need to come not only from China, but also from other countries. Unlike products and capital, talent flows around the world on the basic premise that people must use the common working language of business, and, as revealed by 93% (n=465) of the participants in the research conducted for this chapter, speaking English will enhance their confidence in life and work (see figure 1), with 79% (n=395) of them agreeing that, for the past and present, communicating globally means communicating in English (see figure 2).

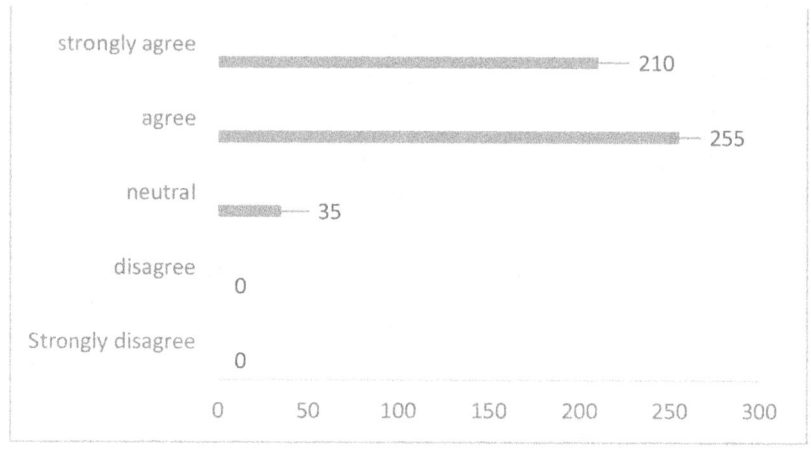

Figure 1. Speaking English can enhance confidence in life and work

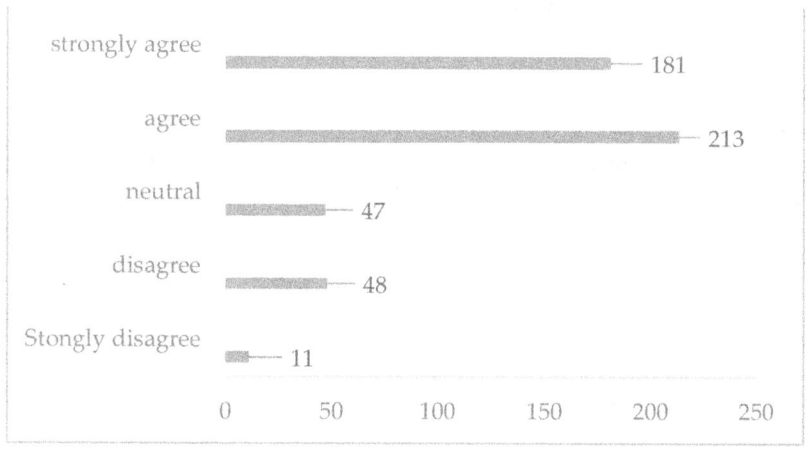

Figure 2. Communicating globally has been communicating in English

Table 2. *Variable correlations*

		English Language Dominance	AI	Rise of Mandarin's Economic Strength
		Variable Correlations		
Pearson Correlation	English Language Dominance	1.000	-0.279	-0.260
	AI	-0.279	1.000	0.617
	Rise of Mandarin's in Economic Strength	-0.260	0.617	1.000
Sig. (1-tailed)	English Language Dominance	0.000	0.000	0.000
	AI	0.000	0.000	0.000
	Rise of Mandarin's Economic Strength	0.000	0.000	0.000
N	English Language Dominance	500	500	500
	AI	500	500	500
	Rise of Mandarin's Economic Strength	500	500	500

English Language Future Parameters

Research for this chapter further explores two diameters to define and measure the factors that influence the dominance of the English language moving into the future (the dependent variable, or DV) with the potential impact of AI powered technologies (the independent variable, or IV), for instance, machine translation and robots with deep learning abilities, against the rise of Mandarins economic strength (IV). Based on previous research findings (Wu, 2019), the researcher carried out a perception survey on 500 random international citizens with basic English acquisition and awareness in order to uncover how the application and future of English may continue within the global context under the fourth industrial revolution. The survey distributed to these participants was designed with Likert scale questions ranked: strongly disagree (value of 1), disagree (value of 2), neutral (value of 3), agree (value of 4) and strongly agree (value of 5).

In survey analysis a 1-tailed significance test ($p=0.000 < 0.05$) indicates negative correlations between the DV and IVs. The more developed the AI technologies, the fewer number of years that it will take to challenge English language's preeminent position; the rise of Mandarins economic strength will also see it be a fewer number of years before the dominance of the English language weakens. Refer to table 2.

AI powered technologies in Industry 4.0

Machine translation and deep learning robots

English nowadays has been formed by the influence of the industrial revolutions. When each industrial revolution began, the world would demonstrate technological discoveries and rapid change of social-economical structures, shaping the hegemony and hierarchical structure of world languages (Goodfellow, Bengio, Courville, 2016). In human history, the use of steam power in 1784 that led to mechanical production marked the first industrial revolution which brought English to the world-dominant status (Wu & Duan, 2018). Mankind experienced two industrial revolutions since then, with the use of electricity in the beginnings of the 20th century enabling mass production in industries bringing the second industrial revolution (Gleason, 2018). The third industrial revolution refers to the pervasive use of Information technologies (IT) since the 1980s. IT has empowered human beings to have remarkably increased automation throughout the entire manufacturing process (Ibid). Right after English became the world's language of discovery and accomplishments at the end of the 20th century manufacturing, materials science, engineering, and communications all led to the requirement of new communicative functions from language. Technology, coming alongside each industrial revolution, also built up legal, management and accounting structures which all provided a great amount of information, and this led employees to then need to cope with developing new skills, and the ability to communicate in a more complex atmosphere (Brybjolfsson & McAfee, 2014).

Indeed, technology has had a profound impact upon language and culture historically. But with the rise of industry 4.0 are we now experiencing the emergence of revolutionary technologies, and ones that will reform our use and perception of language in the way that the previous industrial revolutions did?

The answer is surely yes. Industry 4.0 was proposed by the German government in April 2013 (Wu & Duan, 2018) as the brainchild of safeguarding the future of its leading manufacturing power in global industry, and this marked the start of the fourth industrial revolution. This era is ongoing and disruptive: along with the deepening process of globalization stimulated by trends of connectivity, and it is profoundly service-oriented, with advanced materials coming together with processing technology that can be controlled by computers with collaborative advanced manufacturing network devices. The perfect marriage of advanced materials, technologies and computing networks has contributed to the infinite smartness of physical-digital environments, which is the viral concept of the internet of things (IoT) and artificial intelligence (AI) today. English undergoing new changes, and simplification will be the main developmental trend as the Chinese linguist Zhou (2017) predicts: in the 21st century, English spelling and pronunciation are to be unified gradually, with irregular changes in vocabulary and grammar altered by analogy. He continues to say that the use of abbreviations, ellipsis sentences and short sentences will become increasingly popular; morphological transformation will be very flexible and expression is going to become more concise; repetition rates of common words will be quite high and the distinction between countable and uncountable nouns, transitive and intransitive verbs, and so on, will disappear. All these changes will greatly facilitate in the learning and the use of English as a communicative tool.

Although Industry 4.0 originally aimed to give full play to the traditional advantages of German manufacturing, it provoked revolutionary breakthroughs in a new round of technologies which lead to rapid and significant advances in all walks of life. This has since imposed great impact on the entire world, including affecting our lifestyles, changing the ways in which we look at the world by broadening and deepening our visions, and it also proposes a potential reshape of language hierarchical structure: the languages used by countries that lead the tide of industry 4.0 tend to show preeminence (Huang, 2011).

Thanks to statistical and deep learning techniques, it is also becoming increasingly possible to enable machines to understand and to achieve seamless communication between languages in Industry 4.0. In 2018, Babel Fish earbuds have been included on the list of top 10 MIT-Review breakthrough technologies under the category of gadgets to reinforce learning (MIT Technology Review, 2017). These earbuds can translate what is being said and play it aloud on a smart phone when communicating. After the person with the phone responds, the answer is translated and then played in the earbuds. This technology can translate in real time, it is suitable for multiple languages, and it is easy to use.

The 21st century is an era for artificial intelligence to empower the robotics process of our languages as naturally as human beings. Natural language processing (NLP) is a field at the intersection of computer science, artificial intelligence, and linguistics. The goal is for computers to process and 'understand' natural language in order to perform tasks that are useful like making appointments, buying things, and answering questions – for example, by using Siri, Google Assistant, Facebook M, and Cortana (Goodfellow, Bengio, Courville, 2016). However, fully understanding and representing the meaning of language or even defining it is a demanding goal. Language used to be the most distinctive property of human beings, but the emergence of AI might pose a threat to the survival of English as a global language. AI machine translation technology, or machine natural language processing technology, will one day be able to translate every language into every other language, and it is advancing at an extraordinary speed. So where are we in the era of machine translation now? How do people of the 21st century generation perceive this advancement?

Industry has begun to focus on machine translation. Google, Baidu, Facebook, and other tech-based companies are implementing machine translation and online translation systems, developed with the Google Translator Toolkit, Microsoft LocStudio, and Trados.

It can be seen that with the development of technology, machine translation will have great application in the spaces of education, tourism, social contact, cross-border transactions and other fields (Feng, 2018). Advances in AI technology are constantly lowering the cost of communication for people, and when machine translation advances to the point where it can replace professional translation, it could lead to a world where people of any language can communicate seamlessly. Will this possibility arrive in the near future?

According to the perception questionnaire delivered to participants of the research conducted for this chapter, more than 90% ($n=450$) of the participants think that the increase in the use of AI translation technology will make it unnecessary to learn English. They also perceive that AI machine translation will become as good as human translation (90.6%, $n=453$) and will overtake mediocre human translators (92.4%, $n=462$), that it can be as accurate as human beings in language scales (90.6%, $n=453$), and that it can help to remove language barriers and enhance human beings' communicative abilities (94.8%, $n=474$). It will allow them travel to any part of the world without speaking any of the languages themselves (93%, $n=465$). AI machine translation makes it possible to hear only one's own language in communication (95.2%, $n=476$), and it makes the communication more in-depth and exciting If everyone can communicate in their own language; it would help to preserve languages that aren't as widely spoken as English and other behemoth languages (95%, $n=475$; see figure 3). AI machine translation technologies such as speech recognition, language identification, translation modeling and speech generation are mature enough to allow people to communicate freely (93%, $n=465$), and it can learn as fast as human beings (93.2%, $n=466$; see figure 4).

Rise of China and the Economic Strength of Mandarin

International trade is often a complex, cross-border business: goods are taken from one country, refined or given added value by a second, sold to a third, repackaged, resold, and so on. Such multilateral trade brings with it greater reliance on lingua francas (Graddol, 1997), and today Mandarin is gaining popularity because of its increasing importance in international business trade (Guo & Wu, 2018). It is perhaps becoming inevitable to

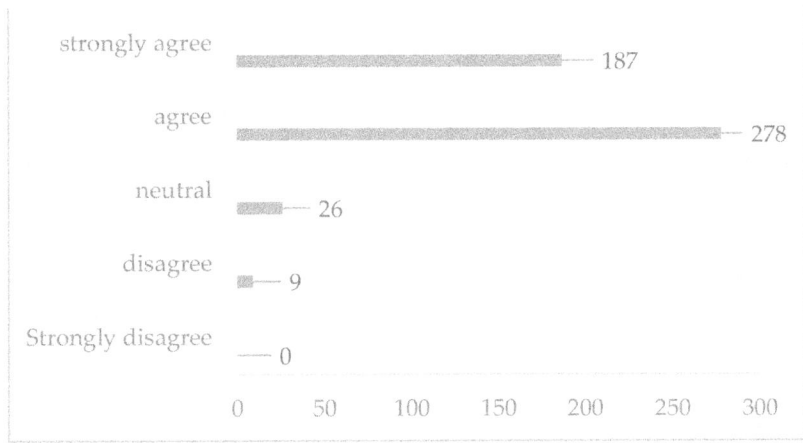

Figure 3. AI machine translation technology is able to preserve languages not widely spoken

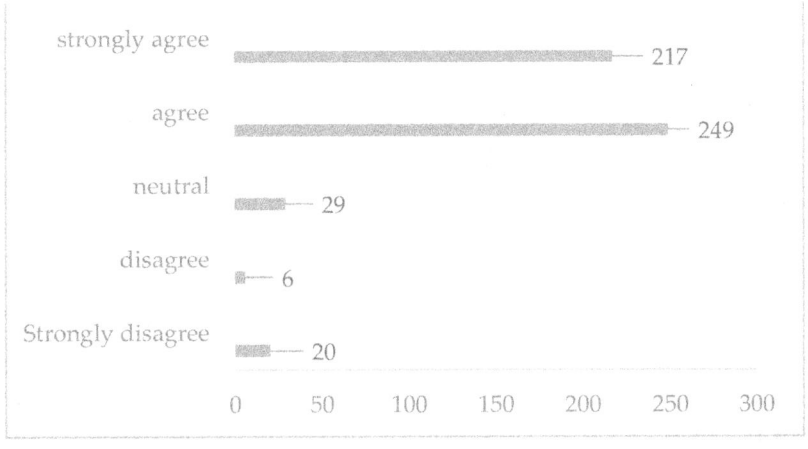

Figure 4. AI machines can learn as fast as human beings

communicate with Chinese businessmen in Mandarin to purchase 'Made in China' products in China or in the Chinese factories located in other countries. Mandarin is also seen to be gaining popularity because of the increasing importance of the PRC in the arena of international politics (Ibid). China's economy continues to perform strongly—with growth that was projected to be 6.6 percent in 2018 (IMF, 2018). Four decades of reform have transformed China from one of the poorest countries in the world to the second largest economy (IMF, 2018). In its latest annual assessment of the Chinese economy, the IMF (2018) predicted that even with a gradual slowdown in growth, China could become the world's largest economy by 2030 and begin to overtake the United States of America (see figure 5). On the other hand, China is also expected to be a global digital leader (Ibid). Although the English language accounted for 80% of computer-based communication in the 1990s, this proportion has since fallen to around 40% in the early 21st century (Hagen, 2013). According to the World Development Indicators database (WDI, 2018), China has around 700 million internet users, and 282 million digital natives (referring to internet users less than 25 years old) who yearn to adopt new skills and technological innovations. On the other hand, the massive scale of the Chinese market and a supportive regulatory and supervisory environment in the early years of digitization has made China a global leader in frontier industries which includes e-commerce and fintech (IMF, 2018; see figure 6). Digitization is expected to reshape the Chinese economy by improving efficiency, softening—but not reversing—slowing growth as the economy matures (Ibid).

Since English is not native for Chinese people, English language has become a common and severe challenge for Chinese enterprises as the working language of globalization. Existing English-speaking economies remain powerful including the United States, Britain, Canada, Australia, let alone that there are many other countries with English as their second language. This forms a great economic strength for the English language. It also gives other former British colonies such as India a huge linguistic advantage in the world business share. By contrast, the fact that Chinese, except for those in Hong Kong, use English as a working language has become a basic problem. If it is the economic forces that have made English the working language of world business,

Will English Remain a Lingua Franca? | 199

with the economic rise of non-English-speaking countries such as China in recent decades, why can't the world's business language be Mandarin? Data from the research for this chapter shows that 91.8% (*n* = 459) of the participants surveyed agree that rise of China and Mandarin Chinese pose a challenge to the dominance of English language (see figure 7).

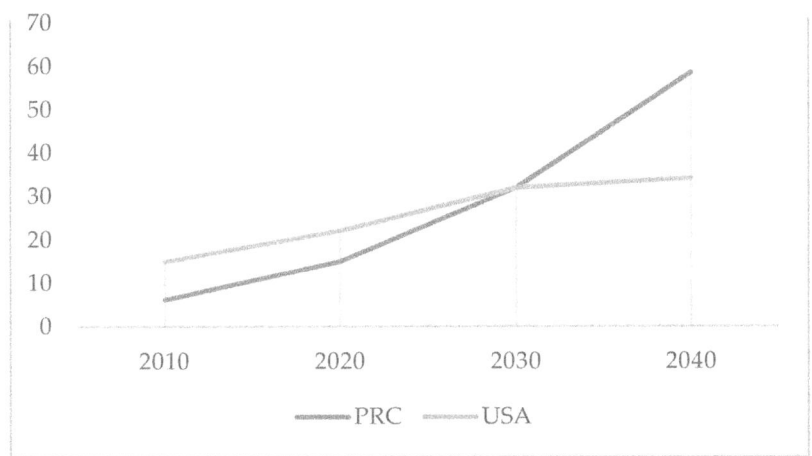

Figure 5. The People's Republic of China (PRC) gross domestic product (GDP) could overtake that of the United States of America (USA) by 2030 (*World Economic Forum, 2019*)

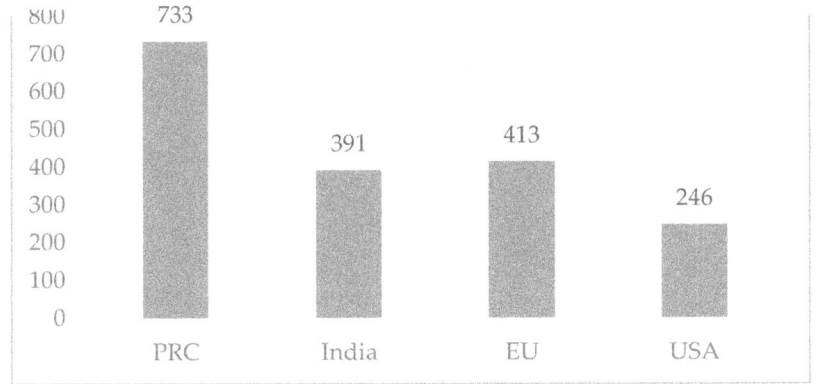

Figure 6. China a global leader in frontier industries (internet users in millions of persons; World Economic Forum, 2019)

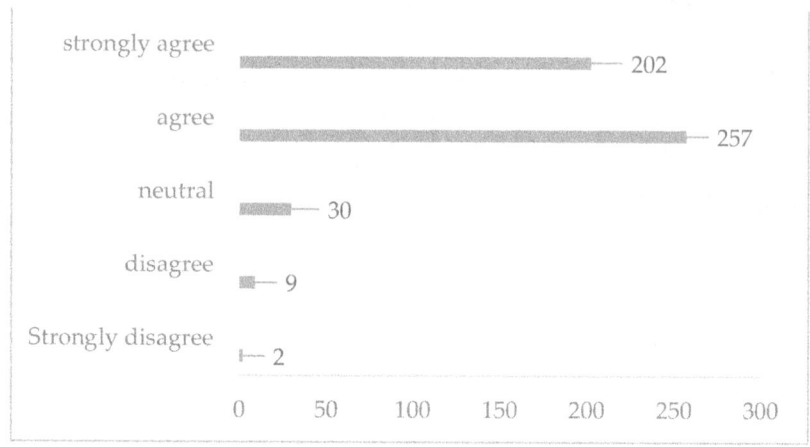

Figure 7. Belief that the rise of Mandarin, in terms of economic strength, poses a challenge to the dominance of English

Leith (2002) put forward the term of 'gross language product' (GLP) to estimate the economic strength of language, which is to divide real data of gross domestic product (GDP) by the population in a country. Table 3, counting the four major English-speaking countries as a whole) illustrates gross domestic product versus gross language product rankings for the year of 2018.

Prediction of the Future of English in the Industry 4.0 Era

How do we understand and establish a linkage between the factors which were discussed previously and the future of the English language worldwide, is actually a process of building and testing a theory?

In this study, a regression model is built based on quantitative data obtained via an electronically delivered perception questionnaire undertaken on 500 individuals' perception of the English language, AI powered machine translation and deep learning technologies, along with their perceptions of the rise of China and the place of Mandarin. The perception questionnaire is available online (www.wenjuan.com/s/viEV3). Participants were scattered across 61 nations and had been more or less exposed to

English language learning for an average of 25.95 years according to the survey data.

Table 3. Gross domestic product versus gross language product rank for the year of 2018

GDP Rank	Country	Major Language	Projected GDP Growth 2018 (%)	Population (in million)	GLP = GDP/Population	GLP Rank
1	The Four Major English Speaking Economies		2.4	453	0.0052974465468816	8
	USA		2.9	325.72		
	UK	English	1.4	66.02		
	Canada		2.1	36.71		
	Australia		3.0	24.60		
2	PRC	Mandarin	6.6	1386.4	0.0047605480406073	9
3	Spain	Spanish	2.8	46.57	0.0601219229653507	1
4	Saudi Arabia	Arabic	1.9	32.94	0.0576837660577184	2
5	India	Hindu	7.3	1339.18	0.0054510964107569	7
6	France	French	1.8	67.12	0.0268181794478882	3
7	Japan	Japanese	1.0	126.79	0.0078873181611390	6
8	Russia	Russian	1.7	144.50	0.0117651097227974	4
9	Brazil	Portuguese	1.8	209.29	0.0086005771560643	5

Note: Date sources are IMF (2018) for GDP data, and The World Bank Group (2019) for population data

The perception questionnaire contains 80 questions which were designed to collect information on the participants' English acquisition, the predictive factors that contribute to English language change over time, and on their perception of artificial intelligence (AI) and its influence on the use and education of English language in the ongoing digital revolution era. The related disruptive AI-powered technologies under discussion are machine translation with deep learning abilities. The data strictly applied in the model for research includes demographics, ordinal (Likert) scales, and numeric data. The study aims to investigate the influence of AI technologies on the participants perception of English language use and education so as to predict whether and when English language could be challenged as the dominant global language.

The author applied SPSS to run the data quantitatively for variables correlation analysis, an independent samples t-test, and an F-test (ANOVA analysis) to investigate whether the hypothetical influencing factors are correlated to English language change and whether the regression mode fits to predict the future of the English language. The research will ultimately apply a multiple linear regression analysis to build on a prediction model which will hopefully yield constructive findings to better predict the future of English and shed some light on the potential reform of English language use and education in the digital revolution period with AI powered innovations. The researcher wishes to regress the dependent variable (DV): In_ years English language dominance will be challenged with Artificial intelligence (AI as an IV) and the rise of Mandarins economic strength (as an IV). Table 4 below is the model summary which reports that the adjusted R Square is 0.087, reporting that a proportion of 8.7% of total variability in DV is explained by the two independent variables. The R Square value is 0.090 which is very close to the adjusted R Square value of 0.087, suggesting neither of the two IVs are redundant in explaining the

DV. In this research, it can be interpreted that using AI-powered technologies and the rise of Mandarins economic strength as independent variables can predict what the future of English is, and this can be further illustrated by the emerging Pearson correlation R value.

Table 4. *Model summary*

Model Summary[b]									
Model	R	R^2	Adjusted R^2	Std. Error of the Estimate	Change Statistics				
					R^2	F	df 1	df 2	Sig. F
1	0.300[a]	0.090	0.087	7.196	0.090	24.640	2	497	0.000

a. Predictors: (Constant), Rise of Chinese in economic strength, AI.
b. Dependent Variable: In_ Years English Language Dominance Will be Challenged.

Table 5 demonstrates the ANOVA statistic F-test with an F value of 24.640 and a *p* value of 0.000, suggesting a very strong significance with a *p* value of 0.000 <0.05, showing strong evidence to reject the null hypothesis. The model therefore has very strong explanatory power.

Table 5. *ANOVA test statistics*

ANOVA[b]						
Model		Sum of Squares	df	Mean Square	F	Sig.
1	Regression	2551.813	2	1275.906	24.640	0.000[a]
	Residual	25735.139	497	51.781		
	TOTAL	28286.952	499			

a. Predictors: (Constant), Rise of Chinese in economic strength, AI
b. Dependent Variable: In_ Years English Language Dominance Will be Challenged

The p values for the model variables in the coefficients table suggest t values of 8.721, -3.519 and -2.607. The significance p values are 0.000, 0.000 and 0.009. Since all p values are smaller than 0.05, which suggests that the coefficients in table 6 therefore present Beta values for constructing the model to predict with significant evidence. Based on the coefficients, the researcher builds a model to predict the future of the English language using the multiple regression equation:

$y = ax_1 + bx_2 + c$

y = In_ years English language dominance will be challenged

x_1 = AI

x_2 = Rise of Mandarin's economic strength

c = constant

English will not Retain its Preeminence in the Industry 4.0 Era
Although language is constantly changing, English is the dominant language among the world's 7,000 languages, its power coming from the rise of Britain and USA in the 19th and 20th centuries. English has many dialects and different accents worldwide due to the colonization hegemony of Britain and USA (Melitz, 2008). Of those surveyed for the research undertaken for this chapter, 93% (n=465) revealed that they feel confident to travel to a country that they have never been to if they speak English because they will be able to talk to more people even though they do not know them (see figure 8).

For the past and present, communicating globally has been communicating in English, and with English being the second language of many countries, working in an international organization requires a strong command of English according to 96% of the surveyed participants. In some countries like India, English is not only a language of communication, but also a language of class and status, with the language becoming an

Table 6. Model coefficients

Coefficients[a]

Model	Unstandardized Coefficients		Standardized Coefficients	t	Sig.	95.0% Confidence Interval for B		Correlations		
	B	Std. Error	Beta			Lower Bound	Upper Bound	Zero-order	Partial	Part
1 (Constant)	41.131	4.716		8.721	0.000	31.865	50.397			
AI	-0.075	0.021	-0.191	-3.519	0.000	-0.117	-0.033	-0.279	-0.156	0.151
Rise of Mandarins economic strength	-0.610	0.234	-0.142	-2.607	0.009	-1.070	-0.150	-0.260	-0.116	0.112

a. Dependent Variable: In_years English language dominance will be challenged

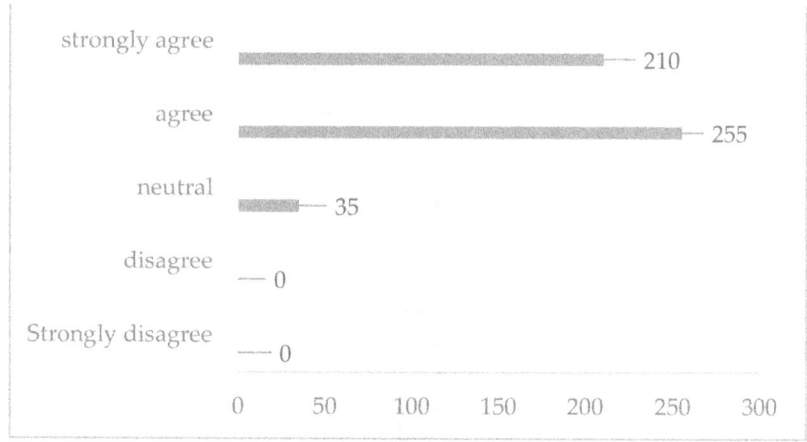

Figure 8. If I speak English, I feel confident
in traveling to a country that I have never visited

essential passport to social acceptance, with proficiency in English viewed an indicator of intelligence to some (BBC News, 2018). In China, English was previously taught to a tiny elite group but now it is taught to a wider range of the general population from a preschool age (Hua & Chen, 2017). It is now taught to a wider range of the general population from preschool age, where parents want their children to gain exposure to English as early as possible in order to provide what they consider to be a better start in life. According to the survey data, 88.6% (n=443) of the participants hold the view that English is going to squeeze out other less-widely spoken languages, with 91.4% (n=457) believing that English will be pushed aside by another language because English is more uniform with the use of the internet. English will be influential among a few very strong languages like Arabic, Hindi-Urdu, Mandarin, and Spanish. On the other hand, English has been fractured by the internet into different interlanguage varieties of the language such as Chinglish (Chinese English), Hinglish (Hindu English) and Konglish (Korean English), and that this trend of hybrid languages poses a threat to English. Meanwhile, the rise of the

PRC and Mandarin poses a challenge to the dominance of English with Mandarin gaining popularity because of its increasing importance in international business trade (Lohmann, 2011). It certainly is easier and more convenient to communicate with Chinese businessmen in Mandarin when purchasing 'Made in China' products in China or in the Chinese factories located in other countries. Mandarin is also seen to be gaining popularity because of the increasing importance of the PRC in the arena of international politics (Guo & Wu, 1028).

AI may be a threat to the survival of English as a global language as its machine translation technology will one day be able to translate every language into every other language. AI technologies are advancing at an extraordinary speed. To some extent, the increased use of machine translation may make it unnecessary to learn any language because machine translation powered by AI will potentially become as good as human translators in terms of language ability scales. It may at some point overtake untrained mediocre human translators and it could perhaps be one day accurate enough to understand complicated and nuanced technical documents and conversations AI innovations can potentially remove language barriers and enhance human beings' communicative abilities, and this will allow us to travel to any part of the world without having to speak any of the local languages. AI machine translation could make it possible to communicate by speaking and hearing only our own language, and communication could become more in-depth and enjoyable accordingly. In terms of this, AI machine translation could help to preserve languages that aren't as widely spoken as English along with the other behemoth languages. AI machine translation technologies such as speech recognition, language identification, translation modeling, and speech generation are already mature enough to allow people to communication freely (K & I Center, 2018). AI machine deep learning methods such as computer vision, speech recognition, natural language processing, audio recognition, social network filtering, and machine translation are powerful in modeling a real-world context. The deep learning ability enables machines to adapt faster than human beings (Goodfellow, Bengio, Courville, 2016). AI disruptive innovation is one of the driving forces that make people feel important when learning English (ye, 2017) because most of the controls and commands of modern electronic devices are in English. Additionally, AI machine deep learning is affecting the way we use languages. Learning a new language takes a massive amount of time and effort and learning it later in life is not the same as learning one's native language (Oster, 2010). So, AI deep learning and machine translation can potentially move us from a single language future to one where we can all rely upon our native language. From those responding to the perception questionnaire distributed for this survey 97% (n=485) hope that, in the future, they will not have to feel the need to learn a language that they did not learn naturally. It should be noted that this is different to wanting to learn about the language and culture of another people. AI disruptive innovation makes English, or potentially any language, less likely to remain as the main language for international communication. AI allows us to use electronic gadgets and smart phones with interfaces in any language that suits us. Recent innovations, like these, have been so disruptive that they are going to revolutionize the way that English (and other languages) are taught (e.g., using the likes of all kinds of online media services such as YouTube, and social media services like those provided by Facebook and Wechat). AI is not only changing our lifestyle but also altering the ways in which we are teaching languages. The idea of radio broadcasts, newspapers, and TV programs being translated and understood no matter what languages they are in would likely excite most people in the world.

AI technologies may soon provide people with the choice of turning away from learning any language, seeing them able to rely upon the use of their native tongue. The advantages that this potentially offers are those that see such speakers free to communicate in their own language with less pressure, and in full command of a natural vocabulary and phraseology. On the other hand, humans may still choose to learn additional languages, such as English, as they may not want to relinquish control over their expression and become dependent upon AI machine translation. However, those surveyed for the research undertaken for this chapter predominantly fancy the idea of AI machine translation, particularly since it carries with it the potential for life to be made easier, and for their thoughts and expressions to be more widely understood (both by humans and machines). In this context too, AI could potentially see the world become more multilingual rather than less so. These aspects are illustrated in table 7.

A hybrid and flexible language
English has always been an evolving language and language contact has been an important driver of change. First from Celtic and Latin, later from Scandinavian and Norman French, and more recently from the many other languages spoken in the former British colonies, the English language has borrowed freely (Steiner, 2001). Analysts, like Hua and Chen (2017), see this hodgepodge and permeability of English as defining features, allowing it to expand quickly into new domains and explaining in part its success as a world language. Today too, Chinglish, Konglish, Hinglish, Spanglish, and so on, are terms that refer to the speaking of language with fractures of English vocabulary and structures being absorbed into many different languages such as Chinese, Korean, Hindi, and Spanish (Grimes, 1996). Others, like Leech (1995), believe that vocabulary and

Table 7. *Perception questions of artificial intelligence on English language*

Perception questions (in part)	Positive Proportion of Likert Scale Answers in Percent (N=500)	Question 22
12. If I learn English, I will be able to talk to more people even though I do not know them.	95.6	
13. If I speak English, I will feel confident when traveling to a country that I have never been to.	93	
14. I think English has many dialects and different people have different accents worldwide.	96.2	
15. Language is constantly changing.	94.8	
16. English is the dominant language among the world's 7,000 languages.	88.4	
17. The power of English comes from the rise of Britain and the USA in the 19th and 20th centuries.	93.8	
18. English will be as influential as a few very strong languages, such as Arabic, Mandarin, Spanish, and Urdu.	90.0	
19. For the past and present, communicating globally has meant communicating in English.	78.8	
20. The second language of many countries is English.	96.6	
69. AI disruptive innovation is going to revolutionize the way that English is taught with the likes of all kinds of online media (e.gh., the use of YouTube or social networking services like WeChat).	95.2	
70. AI disruptive innovation is changing the way in which the teaching of English is done, making it more entertaining.	95.8	
71. AI is changing our lifestyle.	95.2	4
72. The idea of radio broadcasts, newspapers and TV programs being translated and understood no matter what languages they are in makes me feel excited.	95.4	
73. I do not think that, in the future there will be a difference between humans and machines in recognizing either voice or discourse text.	92.0	
74. I no longer have to learn by traditional means of communication to participate in the world thanks to AI machine translation.	91.0	
75. I feel more identity through the use of my own traditional language without, at the same time, losing the advantages of being in touch with people through other languages.	94.6	
76. The more I am free to speak my own language, the less pressure I fell with having a global language for me to communicate in.	91.8	
77. I feel that in the AI future, languages will just become tools of communication.	92.0	
78. I feel that there is still a need to learn English because I want to have control over expressing myself rather than become dependent on AI machine translation to do it for me.	96.4	
79. I like the idea of AI machine translation as it can make my life easier and my own language more widely understood by computers.	96.2	
80. AI will make the world more multilingual rather than less so.	94.4	

grammatical structures of spoken English will be simplified to the maximum extent with continued use and the development of the internet and online social media applications for communication.

One of the few certainties associated with the future of English is that it will likely continue to evolve, reflecting and constructing the changing roles and identities of its speakers. Yet we are now at a significant point of evolution: at the end of the 20th century, the close relationship that has previously existed between language, territory, and cultural identity is being challenged by globalizing forces (Gong & Fan, 2000). The impact of such trends will shape the contexts in which English is learned and used in the 21st century.

Speakers of English as second or foreign language outnumber first (native) language speakers

Based on the perception questionnaire data, the English-speaking population will still be increasing but there is a decreasing trend of learning enthusiasm for English due to convenience and accuracy brought by AI machine translation technologies. The British Broadcast Corporation reported in June of 2018, that one in five people in the contemporary world speaks English (BBC News, 2018), which suggests that there is room for many more speakers to learn it, and it is estimated that one third of the world population will be speaking English by 2030 (Crystal, 2005). In line with these figures 18.8% of respondents to the perception questionnaire, disseminated to 500 random participants for this research, are native speakers of the English language.

A flexible multilingual future world is coming alongside AI technology

Those who speak English alongside other languages outnumber English native speakers, and this provides significant implications for a flexible multilingual future world. Based on the perception questionnaire data, 84% ($n=420$) of those surveyed speak at least 2 languages, and 16% ($n=79$) speak 3 or more languages (see figure 9). Statistics show that the more languages these people speak, the less willing they are to learn English and the more willing they are to embrace an AI-powered multilingual world where machines allow them to speak their own languages for communicative purposes.

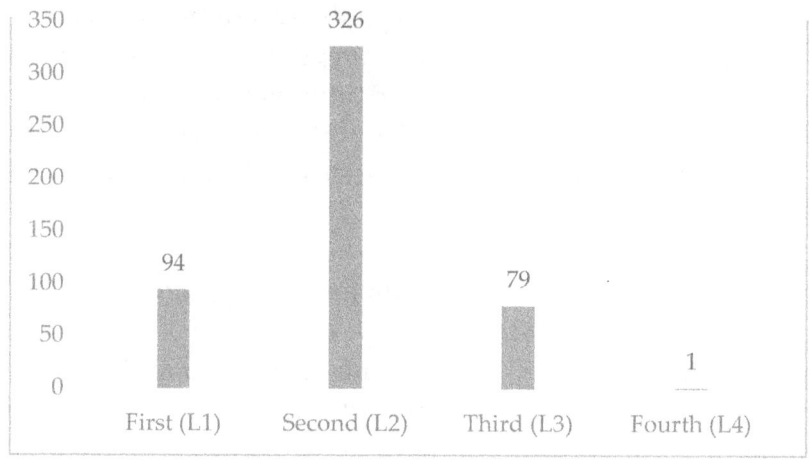

Figure 9. Speakers of English as first (L1), second (L2), third (L3) and fourth languages (L4)

Language primary function shift from a carrier of culture to communication

Today, more people perhaps value English as a communication medium than ever before, but the traditional function of a language is as a representative and carrier of regional culture (Emily, 2015). English enjoyed its preeminence in the 19th and 20th centuries with the British and the American hegemony status on the world stage, and it is natural for English to have spread the core values and cultures of these two English-speaking countries. However, in this century, now that machine translation technologies are available to translate every language into another (although sometimes questionable as to how good), people (K & I Center, 2018) are doubting the necessity of a lingua franca, instead, they call for a powerful technology to facilitate communication and to better present their local culture and values which were previously perceived to be peripheral (Large, 1985). Many perception questionnaire participants (94.6%, $n=473$) revealed that they can not only engage in a more thorough and detailed conversation but that they can also maintain more of their identity when using their native tongue to communicate (see figure 10).

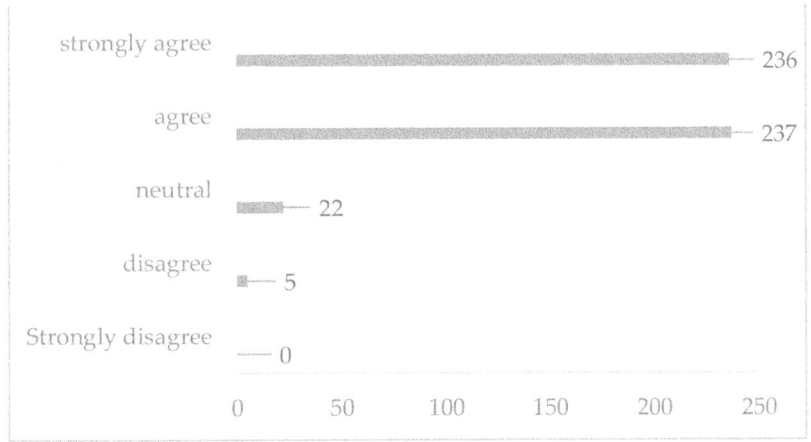

Figure 10. Identity perception data
for using native tongue to communicate

Discussion and Conclusion

Language is in constant change, and the economic strength of Mandarin has come along with the rise of China on the world stage in the 21st century (Zhou, 2017). This research has shown that the dominant position of the English language as a global language is being challenged. The deeper and wider communication via internet and social-economical globalization has made English develop in two contradictory directions. In grammar and structure, it went increasingly astray with the generative grammar which regulates and encourages norms. English is presenting more communicative-oriented characteristics both phonetically and lexically coinciding with the diversified and flexible tendencies required by regional dialects and varieties, many of which had gradually evolved into separate languages with national identities in history (Leech, 1995). Meanwhile, with the prevalence of AI-powered technologies and machine translation, English is no longer desired as the only media language for communication due to the increasing possibility of all speakers to rely upon their native languages for communication. People may then value their own languages more than that of English, seeing the world maintain linguistic diversity.

Ultimately this research predicts that in less than a decade from now (9.46 years to be exact, according to the perception questionnaire data; see figure 11 and table 8) the speaking of English language by those that may choose to learn it, will likely be completely replaced by AI powered robots and machine translation. Yet, we still as humans have a choice. Do we want to be reliant on machine translation for all our communication?

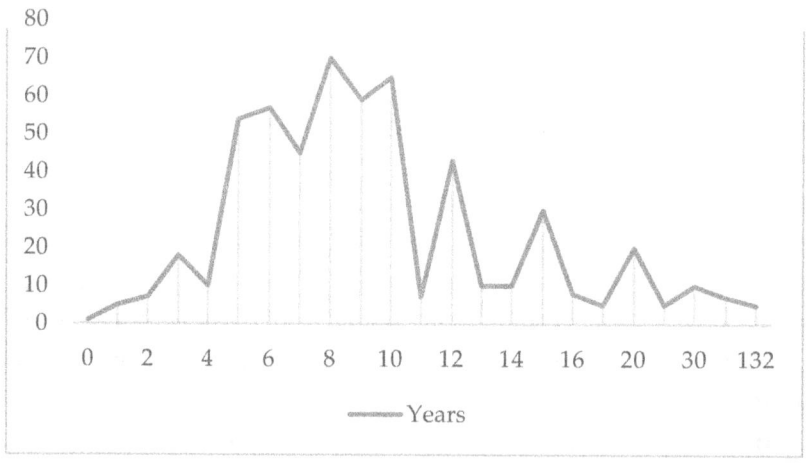

Figure 11. In_ years English language dominance will be challenged by AI

Table 8. *In_ years English language dominance will be challenged by AI*

In_ Years English Language Dominance will be challenged by AI						
	N	Min.	Max.	Mean	SD	
	Statistic	Statistic	Statistic	Statistic	Std. Error	Statistic
Q11_open	500	0	100	9.46	0.285	6.372
Valid N	500					

References

Albert H., & Xiao Y. (2007). Pronunciation and grammar of future English. *Foreign Languages Teaching, 3*, 35-41.

BBC News. (2018, March 23). *Compass: From language to algorithm.* British Broadcasting Corporation World Service.

Bond, F., Oepen, S., Nicholas, E., Flickinger, D., Velldal, E., & Haugereid, P. (20100). Deep open-source machine translation. *Machine Translation, 25*(2), 87-105.

Brynjolfsson, E., & McAfee, A. (2014). *The second machine age: Work, progress, and prosperity in a time of brilliant technologies.* New York, USA: W. W. Norton.

Coulmas. F. (2012). Attractiveness of Japanese language, *Japanese Linguistics and Literature, 7*, 87-99.

Crystal, D. (1997). *English as a global language.* Cambridge, UK: Cambridge University Press.

Crystal, D. (2005). *Cambridge encyclopedia of the English language.* Cambridge: Cambridge University Press.

Graddol, D. (1997). *The future of English? A guide to forecasting the popularity of the English language in the 21st century.* London, United Kingdom: The English Company Ltd

Emily, U. (2015). *The search for the perfect language.* Oxford: Blackwell.

Feng, C. (2018). Big data and artificial intelligence empower English teaching and learning. *Chinese Education Journal, 5*, 105-123.

Finneran, K. (1987). Future of English. *World Science, 11*, 48-50.

Firth, A. (1996). "Lingua Franca" English and conversation analysis. *Journal of Pragmatics, 4*(5), 32-48.

Gleason, N. (Ed.). (2018). *Higher education in the era of the fourth industrial revolution*. USA: Palgrave Macmillan.

Gong X, & Fan C. (2000). The motive and approach of language development: English today and tomorrow. *Journal of HUST· Social Science Edition, 14*(1), 56-62.

Goodfellow, I., Bengio, Y., & Courville, A. (2016). *Deep learning*. USA: MIT Press.

Grimes, B. (1996). *Ethnologue: Languages of the world*. Dallas: Summer Institute of Linguistics.

Guo, J., & Wu, Y. H. (2018). A quantitative study of the development of the Confucius Institute during 2015-2017. *Journal of Yunan Normal University (Humanities and Social Sciences), 50*(5), 36-44.

Hagen, S. (2003). *Languages in European business: A regional survey of small and medium-sized companies*. London: CILT.

Hagen, P. (2013). *Languages in the 21st Century*. Urbana, USA: University of Illinois Press.

Hua, L., & Chen L. (2017). Artificial intelligence reforms English learning. *Modern Distant Education, 6*, 27-31.

Hunag, X., Acerd, A., & hon, H. (2011). *Spoken Language Processing: A guide to theory, algorithm, and system development*. USA: Prentice Hall.

IMF. (2018, July 16). *World economic outlook update*. Washington, DC. USA: International Monetary Fund. Retrieved from https://www.imf.org/en/Publications/WEO/Issues/2018/07/02/world-economic-outlook-update-july-2018

K & I Center. (2018). *AI machine translation research report*. Research Series, 5. PRC: Qinghua Chinese Engineering Institute.

Kachru, B. (1985). Standards, codification and sociolinguistic realism: The English language in the outer circle. In R. Quirk, & H. Widdowson. (Eds.), *English in the world* (pp. 11-30). Cambridge, UK: Cambridge University Press.

Krauss, M. (1992). The world's languages in crisis. *Language, 68*(1), 7-9.

Large, A. (1985). *The artificial language movement*. Oxford, UK: Blackwell publishing.

Leech. G. (1995). Past, present and future of English grammar. *Foreign Linguistics and Research, 2,* 60-80.

Leith, D. (1996). English – Colonial to postcolonial. In D. Graddol, D. Leith, and J. Swann (Eds.), *English: history, diversity and change* (pp. 180-221). London, UK: Routledge.

Liu, Y. (2016). English is not likely to be the only global language in the future. *China Social Science Journal, 3,* 76-82.

Lohmann, J. (2011). Do language barriers affect trade? *Economics Letters, 110,* 137-152.

McArthur, T. (1992). (Ed.). *The Oxford companion to the English language*. Oxford, UK: Oxford University Press.

McArthur, T. (1996). English in the world and in Europe. In R. Hartmann (Ed.), *The English language in Europe* (pp. 3-12). Oxford: Intellect.

Melitz, J. (2008). Language and foreign trade. *European Economic Review, 52(4),* 667-699.

MIT Technology Review. (2017). *MIT Technology Review Names the Top 10 Breakthrough Technologies of 2017*. Retrieved from https://www.highsnobiety.com/2017/02/23/mit-technology-review-2017

Myers-Scotton, C. (2009). Code-switching with English: Types of switching, types of communities. *World Englishes, 8*(3), 333–346.

Oster, N. (2010). *The last lingua franca*. Oxford: Oxford University Press.

Qian, Y. (2006). Keynote speech. Global Entrepreneurship Summit. Retrieved from http://www.sohu.com/a/120436101_534357

Skudlik, S. (1992). The status of German as a language of science and the importance of the English language for German-speaking scientists. In U. Ammon and M. Hellinger (Eds.), *Status change of languages* (pp. 391-407). Berlin, Germany: Walter de Gruyter.

Steiner, G. (2001). *After Babel: Aspects of language and translation.* Oxford, UK: Oxford University Press.

The World Bank Group. (2019). *Population, total.* World Development Indicators Database. Retrieved from https://data.worldbank.org/indicator/SP.POP.TOTL

Viereck, W. (1996). English in Europe: Its nativization and use as a lingua franca, with special reference to German-speaking countries. In R. Hartmann (Ed.), *The English language in Europe* (pp. 16-23). Oxford: Intellect.

Wan, H. (2015). On the analysis of hierarchical economic strength of language. *Theory Journal, 5*(255), 124-130.

Webster, N. (1789). An essay on the necessity, advantages and practicability of reforming the mode of spelling, and of rendering the orthography of words correspondent to the pronunciation. Appendix to Dissertations on the English Language. Extracts reprinted in T. Crowley (Ed.) *Proper English: readings in language, history and cultural identity*. London: Routledge.

World Economic Forum. (2019). This is what China's economy looks like in 2018 – in 6 charts. International Monetary Fund. Retrieved from https://www.weforum.org/agenda/2018/08/china-s-economic-outlook-in-six-charts

Wu, Y. (2019). Will English Language remain unassailable with the rise of Chinese and AI in industry 4.0? *The Journal of Modern China Studies, 21*, 78-97.

Wu, Y., Duan Y. C. (2018). "Made in China": Building Chinese Smart Manufacturing Image. *Journal of Service Science and Management, 11*(6), 590-608.

Wu. Y., Kam. I. (2018). Note-taking Assisted with Computers-A Practical Method to Build a Connection between Chinese Pinyin & Characters. *Chinese Studies, 7*(4), 328-342.

Ye, Y. (2017). On the application and market potential of artificial intelligence in auxiliary learning program: Speaking fluent English. *Chinese Strategic Emerging Industries, 48,* 119-121.

Zhang, W. (2016). Economic power of English: The impact of English aptitude of Chinese citizens on foreign trade. *International Trade, 8,* 47-55.

Zhou, H. (2017, August, 24). *21st Century Weekly.*

Glossary

AI	Artificial intelligence
APA	American psychological association
BBC	British Broadcasting Corporation
BYOD	Bring your own device
CA	Conversational agents
CACD	Computer assisted classroom discussion
CALL	Computer assisted language learning
COTS	Commercial-off-the-shelf
CPS	Cyber physical systems
CD	Compact disc
CMC	Computer mediated communication
DGBLL	Digital game-based language learning
DLL	Digital language learning
DV	Dependent variable
DVD	Digital versatile disc
EFL	English as a foreign language
ESL	English as a second language
GDP	Gross domestic product
GLP	Gross language product
HTML	Hypertext mark-up language
IMF	International Monetary Fund
IT	Information technology
IoT	Internet of things
IV	Independent variable
L1	First language
L2	Second language
LMS	Learner management system
MA TESOL	Master of arts in the teaching of English to speakers of other languages
MALL	Multimedia assisted language learning
MLA	Modern language association
MOOC	Massive open online courses
NLP	Natural language processing
NMT	Neural machine translation
OWL	Online writing lab

PC	Personal computer
PLE	Personal learning environment
RALL	Robot assisted language learning
RSS	Real simple syndication
SNS	Social networking site
STEM	Science technology engineering mathematics
TBLT	Task based language teaching
TELL	Technology enhanced language learning
TESOL	Teaching English to speakers of other languages
TESOL-MALL	The acronym for the graduate level language teacher education program at Woosong University in the Republic of Korea
TIE	Technology integration evaluation
TIER	Technology integration evaluation rubric
URL	Uniform resource locator
VR	Virtual reality
ZDD	Zone of distal development
ZPD	Zone of proximal development

About the Book

Key to the provision of education in the era of the fourth industrial revolution is understanding the use and applicability of various technologies with 21st century learners, as well as being able to assess the usability, implementation, and evaluation of any technological tool that an instructor (or learner) may choose to use. As such, this text aims to not only introduce teachers of English to speakers of other languages (TESOL) to the theories behind this topic, but, more importantly, it seeks to present a range of practical means of providing digital language learning and teaching in ways that can benefit instructors and pupils alike. Of significance, content has been specifically developed by both native and non-native English language teachers to encompass a range of methods and approaches, as well as a variety of linguistic outcomes suitable to a range of teaching and learning contexts. These include that of young learners through to young adults, and all those undergoing life-long learning. The book is therefore an essential read for any educator, student, administrator, or stakeholder involved with the TESOL industry, particularly those who want to understand how pre-service and in-service teachers are honing their technological teaching craft, and how digital language learning and teaching currently, and will potentially, impact the educational sector.

About the Editor

David Kent is an Associate Professor in the Endicott College of International Studies at Woosong University in the Republic of Korea. He provides teacher education through the TESOL-MALL graduate program where he currently serves as Head of Department.

David is a long-standing member of the academic community with a principal research focus that revolves around digital language learning. He has been living and teaching in Korea since 1995.

He has published a number of books, including *Teaching with Technology: Integrating Technology into the TESOL Classroom*, *Internet in Education: Integrating the Internet into the TESOL Classroom*, and a *TESOL Strategy Guide* series that focuses on the use of specific digital tools for teaching. He has also authored a number of multimedia applications.

Currently, David serves on the editorial board of several journals, and his research articles have been published at the SCOPUS and SSCI levels in such periodicals as *Teaching English with Technology*, *The Journal of Asia TEFL*, and the prestigious *Language Learning and Technology*.

www.ingramcontent.com/pod-product-compliance
Lightning Source LLC
Chambersburg PA
CBHW032040150426
43194CB00006B/363